Addressing Cultural and Linguistic Diversity in Special Education

ISSUES AND TRENDS

Shernaz B. García, Editor

Library of Congress Catalog Card Number 94-69098

ISBN 0-86586-258-3

A Publication of the Division for Culturally and Linguistically Diverse Exceptional Learners, a division of The Council for Exceptional Children.

Copyright 1994 by The Council for Exceptional Children, 1920 Association Drive, Reston, Virginia 22091-1589.

Stock No. D5086

Printed in the United States of America

10 9 8 7 6 5 4 3 2 1

Contents

Preface

With this book, the Division for Culturally and Linguistically Diverse Exceptional Learners (DDEL) is pleased to launch its first major publication devoted to cultural and linguistic diversity in special education. In keeping with the stated goal of the division to publish a monograph on a topic of concern to professionals serving multicultural populations in special education, the DDEL Publications Committee first met in 1991 to select a topic and establish publication policies and procedures for its newly created division. The selection of topics for this monograph was guided by DDEL's mission to promote the welfare and education of exceptional children and youth from diverse ethnic, linguistic, and cultural heritages. Moreover, the committee strongly favored the publication of articles that would move special education research and practice closer to defining effective programs and services for these diverse groups of exceptional learners.

For its first publication, the Publications Committee was committed to being as inclusive as possible of the racial, ethnic, and linguistic diversity reflected among exceptional learners in school and community settings. With this in mind, we felt that a collection of papers would most effectively address the theme from the various perspectives of the four major ethnic groups—African American, American Indian, Asian/Pacific Islander, and Hispanic. We recognize that each of these terms is a collective label that does not adequately recognize the diversity within it. However, this approach provides a starting point, and it suggests that we need a dialogue within DDEL as to how we can more appropriately address this issue in future publications. In spite of several efforts to be more representative, the Publications Committee was unable to secure for publication at this time a paper that included an American Indian perspective. The effort to do so partially explains the delay in getting this book to press.

Achieving adequate representation within and among our publications and in our other efforts continues to be an important and guiding consideration for DDEL. For the first time in the history of CEC, our division formalizes efforts to provide a forum for all professionals who serve culturally and linguistically diverse exceptional children, youth, and adults. The changing demography underscores the critical need to focus attention upon special education service delivery for this population of students. DDEL is one of CEC's fastest growing divisions and an important source of knowledge in these areas. CEC's commitment to human rights is a cornerstone of its existence as an advocate for individuals with disabilities. To continue to be successful in this mission, it is necessary for us to operate from a perspective that is equally well grounded in cultural and linguistic competence.

Shernaz B. García
Editor

Acknowledgments

As DDEL's first Publications Chair and the editor of this monograph, I wish to acknowledge that my responsibilities in both areas have been greatly supported by the opportunities DDEL provided, and continues to provide, for my professional growth. I must confess I found the task to be challenging at times, primarily because of my own inexperience in these roles at the national level. In addition to the typical activities involved, the Publications Committee was engaged in the business of developing a monograph as well as determining the scope of our activities and operational procedures for their implementation. Consequently, the completion of this monograph also documents DDEL's potential to provide leadership development. My participation within CEC as a DDEL representative reinforces that we, culturally and linguistically diverse special educators, are an underrepresented group—particularly at the leadership level. There is a need for more growth and development opportunities to be made available. In my own case, I am deeply appreciative of that support.

Several people contributed to the development and publication of this monograph. I would particularly like to recognize and thank the individuals listed below, whose expertise, assistance, guidance, and support provided direction to my efforts and furthered my learning and experience in the editorial and publishing arenas. Of special note, my deepest appreciation to Gladys Clark-Johnson, then DDEL president, who communicated trust and confidence in my ability to fulfill my responsibilities.

The DDEL Publications Committee

Nancy Cloud
Mary Crum-González
Marilyn Johnson
Elba Maldonado-Colón
James M. Patton

Reviewers

Gladys Clark-Johnson
Kayte Fearn
Sandra Fradd
John L. Johnson
Marilyn Johnson
Reginald Jones
Millicent I. Kushner
Jacqueline Mault
Jeanette Misaka
Alba A. Ortiz
Bruce Ramírez
Cheryl Y. Wilkinson
James R. Yates

CEC Publications Staff

Jean Boston
Carolyn Boyle

Finally, and most important, to the authors whose work is published here: Thank you for your patience and understanding.

S.B.G.

CHAPTER 1

Education Reform and Service Delivery to African-American Students

Festus E. Obiakor
Bob Algozzine
Bridgie Ford

A fundamental aim of education in American society is individual and collective growth. Since achieving this goal has been at the heart of most educational reforms, it is no surprise that educators are consistently challenged to respond to quality and equity in education (Carnegie Forum on Education and the Economy, 1986; Committee for Economic Development, 1985; Holmes Group, 1988; National Commission on Excellence in Education, 1983). In the seductiveness of reform lie two related concerns. First, educators have fallen prey to the kind of "hard-sell" mentality that often accompanies reform movements (Cuban, 1984, 1990; Kaufman, Kameenui, Birman, & Danielson, 1990). Second, there is a constant search for easy solutions rather than "hard thinking that brings about advances in theory, application, and practice" (Kaufman et al., 1990, p. 114). The General Education Initiative, a reform-related movement aimed at individual and collective growth of students with special needs, has permeated special education literature recently. This chapter focuses on issues related to education reform as embodied in the General Education Initiative and service delivery to African-American students with disabilities.

PERSPECTIVES ON THE GENERAL EDUCATION INITIATIVE

Opinions about research on identification practices; the effects of labeling; teachers' attitudes, skills, and priorities; and the effects of the excellence in education movement have stimulated some professionals to seriously question the appropriateness of classifying and placing some students in special education classrooms for the majority of their education experiences. A seminal perspective describing the concerns and alternative courses of action was presented in a position paper titled "Educating Students with Learning Problems: A Shared Responsibility" (Will, 1986). The following points are noteworthy:

1. The intent to limit the universe of students being discussed was obvious and intentional. The focus was primarily on mild learning problems, but students with severe disabilities were also recognized.

2. There was no intention to pull services away from people in need, and there was no failure to recognize the unserved. In addition to acknowledging that large numbers of students with disabilities were placed in special classes in recent years, the broad group of students in need of special education was also discussed.

3. Although much had been accomplished in special education programs, the perspective that much remained to be done was the primary position taken. Adapting the general education environment was seen as the method for solving the problems facing special education in the next century.

As Will pointed out, "The basic educational issue for serving this growing group of young people is not finding something to call them so we can put money in a pot with that label on it. The basic issue is providing an educational program that will allow them to learn better" (p. 21). A position on developing partnerships and integrating students with disabilities to meet their special learning needs was not particularly radical, but it generated considerable professional debate.

Some of the arguments against sharing responsibilities for educating students with disabilities in general classrooms center on issues related to integration and the right to treatment. The *integration arguments* are based on concerns that some students with disabilities are not overidentified groups in special education. Advocates of these positions believe that general classrooms may be the most appropriate places for many students with disabilities to receive their education, but they argue that research clearly does not support the assertion that all students can be managed and taught effectively in general classes (Braaten, Kauffman, Braaten, Polsgrove, & Nelson, 1988; Walker & Bullis, 1991). They also believe that expecting general education teachers to welcome, successfully teach and manage, and tolerate the most disruptive students is extremely naive and illogical, both from the viewpoint of common sense and from the perspective of available research (Fuchs, Fuchs, Fersntrom, & Hohn, 1991).

The *right to treatment arguments* are based on opinions about eligibility for services, rights to privacy, and appropriate interventions. Some opponents of the principles embodied in the General Education Initiative believe that students with disabilities are underidentified and that under alternative educational initiatives even more will be denied appropriate help (Braaten et al., 1988; Walker & Bullis, 1991). They also argue that being served in special class settings affords some students privacy that they welcome in dealing with their problems (the "segregation is better than integration" argument), and they believe that research does not support the contention that the complex interventions appropriate for use with some students with disabilities can be used effectively in general education settings (Braaten et al., 1988; Fuchs et al., 1991; Kauffman, Cullinan, & Epstein, 1987; Kauffman & Lloyd, 1992; Walker & Bullis, 1991).

The principles embodied in the General Education Initiative involve four fundamental changes in the ways in which special education would be provided (Davis & Maheady, 1990). First, students with learning problems would receive more instruction in general as opposed to special education settings. Second, general, compensatory, and special education teachers would work collaboratively to provide special education in integrated settings. Third, all instructional resources (i.e., financial, educational, and personnel) would be pooled under a single administrator. Fourth, administrative policies and procedures would be developed to encourage placement of students with special learning needs in general classes.

Unfortunately, empirical study of problems associated with these principles has been sparse, and what has been done has been criticized for ignoring important constituencies (e.g., teachers, students, administrators). For example, McKinney and Hocutt (1988) pointed out that "regular educators, who constitute the largest single group to be affected by these proposals, have not had significant input" (p. 15), and Kauffman, Gerber, and Semmel (1988) added that "data reflecting attitudes of regular classroom teachers toward proposed changes in the structure of general and regular education" have been "conspicuously absent" from literature supporting the General Education Initiative (p. 9).

Fuchs and Fuchs (1991) framed the controversies surrounding the integration movement as a debate between abolitionists (those who argue for elimination or reduction of special education alternatives) and conservationists (those who wish to preserve special education's current structure). They expressed the belief that the contrasting perspectives are based on differing levels and types of experiences with general education and differing opinions about the ways and means of achieving important educational goals. For example, they argued that conservationists' skepticism is based on "observation of many educators' unwillingness or inability to work with [mildly disabled] children"; on "blatant intolerance, and sometimes visceral dislike expressed by many teachers toward them"; and on "arbitrary and adamant refusals to permit the return of these pupils, even part time, to their classrooms" (p. 20). Relative to goals, they contrasted the social and attitudinal interests expressed by abolitionists with the academic concerns of conservationists.

Most recently, the arguments about where students with disabilities should be educated have become the basis for heated debate on "inclusion," "full inclusion," and "inclusionary practices" (Ysseldyke, Algozzine, & Thurlow, 1992). Again, conservationists maintain that decisions should be made on an individual basis and that placements outside general education classes are sometimes appropriate (Fuchs & Fuchs, 1991; Hallenbeck, Kauffman, & Lloyd, 1993). Abolitionists focus on home schools as primary environments for special education delivery (Stainback & Stainback, 1991).

AFRICAN-AMERICAN STUDENTS AND SPECIAL EDUCATION

A *Field of Dreams* mentality (i.e., "If we build it they will come") has come to justify the existence of separate special education for many students who may not need it. While the debate about and concern for restructuring education have apparently done justice to the plight of some students who are at risk (e.g., those with behavioral disorders), the undergirding principle of *inclusive* programs to allow for maximization of full potential remains a problem for many African Americans, who represent a large percentage of those placed in special education programs. While the reform rhetoric continues, perspectives on educating students from diverse ethnic and racial backgrounds remain to some extent unchanged (Algozzine, Maheady, Sacca, O'Shea, & O'Shea, 1990; Braaten et al., 1988; Byrnes, 1990; Davis, 1989, 1990; Jenkins, Pious, & Jewell, 1990; Lieberman, 1990; Lilly, 1986; Reynolds, Wang, & Walberg, 1987; Stainback & Stainback, 1984; Will, 1986; Ysseldyke, Algozzine, & Thurlow, 1992).

History Has Not Been Kind

African-American students with special needs have been faced with the following multidimensional problems in school programs:

- The misuse of standardized instruments in judging intelligence and using them inappropriately to categorize people (Anrig, 1985; Hilliard, 1989; Samuda, 1975).

- The unproductive perception that they have "low" or "negative" self-concept because they are experiencing failure in school programs (Obiakor & Alawiye, 1990; Princes & Obiakor, 1990).

- The insufficiency of realistic role models (e.g., African-American teachers) who understand their history, symbols, cultural values, and learning styles (American Association of Colleges for Teacher Education, 1987; Harvey & Scott-Jones, 1985; Ogbu, 1988, 1990; Staples, 1984).

- The lack of multiethnic education to foster cultural acceptance and diversity (Banks, 1977, 1986; Gay, 1980).

In recent years, efforts to address broad educational reform have stressed excellence in education, with an incessant quest for higher test scores, while downplaying inclusiveness, common sense, and practical perspectives (Cummins, 1989; Lauderdale, 1987; Stedman, 1987). This quest for higher test scores legitimizes the monocultural mentality that landmark court actions (e.g., *Brown v. State Board of Education*, 1954) sought to combat. Corder and Quisenberry (1987) noted that "during the first half of the 20th century, courts were kept busy deciding the constitutionality of educational issues in regard to black Americans" (p. 156). Other monumental legal and legislative efforts have addressed unidimensionality by mandating that schools meet the needs of individuals with disabilities irrespective of race, color, gender, or national origin.

The 1964 Civil Rights Act, the 1965 Elementary and Secondary Education Act (ESEA), the 1970 *Diana versus California School Board* case, the 1972 *Miller versus Board of Education, Washington D.C.* case, the 1973 Section 504 of the Vocational Rehabilitation Act (Public Law 93-112), and the 1975 Education for All Handicapped Children Act (Public Law 94-142) are among the most noteworthy examples.

Despite all this activity, the conclusion that the "more things change, the more they stay the same" may be warranted. For example, Jackson (1988) listed the entrenched problems that are correlates of overrepresentation of African Americans in special education programs, underrepresentation of African Americans in gifted programs, and biased assessment of African Americans in general classroom programs. They are:

1. Loss of teaching and administrative jobs by blacks through dismissals, demotions, or displacement.

2. Loss of racial models, heroes, and authority figures for black children.

3. Loss of cherished school symbols, programs, and names of schools by black children when their schools were closed and they were shifted to white schools.

4. Subjection to segregated classes and buses, and exclusion from extracurricular activities.

5. Suspension and expulsion of disproportionate numbers of black students.

6. Exposure of black children to hostile attitudes and behavior of white teachers and parents.

7. Victimization by forced one-way busing policies and the uprooting of black children for placement in hostile school environments.

8. Victimization by misclassification in special education classes and tracking systems.

9. Victimization by unfair discipline practices and arbitrary school rules and regulations.

10. Victimization by ignorance of black children's learning styles and cultural, social, educational, and psychological needs. (p. 455)

Earlier, Staples (1984) stated that "the ideology of equal opportunity masks the reality of a country stratified along racial, gender, and class lines" (p. 2). He decried what he called the *new racism*, which (a) tends to deny the existence of racism or the responsibility for it, (b) defends phony meritocracy, and (c) relies on standardized tests that are not valid predictors of quality performance. It appears that basic concepts assured in efforts to provide free, appropriate education have been dismissed as unimportant or ignored altogether by service providers meeting the needs of African-American students, especially those with special learning needs (cf. Obiakor, 1992; Ysseldyke & Algozzine, 1990; Ysseldyke, Algozzine, & Thurlow, 1992).

The following concerns are foremost among those related to the General Education Initiative:

• Providing free and appropriate public education.

• Identifying the atypical student in a nondiscriminatory manner.

• Using fair procedural safeguards.

• Assessing in nondiscriminatory fashion.

• Placing students in the least restrictive environment.

• Maintaining confidential information.

• Developing and implementing individualized education programs.

• Continuing the evaluation of programs to permit necessary changes.

These concerns translate into a set of questions that must be addressed if significant changes are to occur: Will African-American special students continue to receive unfair treatment in restructured special education settings? Will they return to learn or function in "unhealthy" general classrooms where their plight began? Will they not be included in some school programs? Answers to these questions will be shaped by perspectives taken from research and contemporary practices.

African-American students are likely to differ interindividually and and intraindividually in learning and test-taking skills, as do their white counterparts (Minton & Schneider, 1980). Is it not inappropriate to test and place African-American students using tests that have been standardized with an ethnocentric, white, middle-class sample? Many of these tests produce reliable or consistent results even when they do not measure what they purport to measure. Anrig (1985) warned that "excellence must not become the new code word for a retreat from equity, just when the struggles of recent years are beginning to pay dividends" (p. 623). Environmental factors such as nutrition, self-concept, motivation, anxiety, examiner race, test sophistication, and language have been found to affect academic and test performance (Gould, 1981; Hilliard, 1975, 1989; Obiakor, 1990, 1991; Obiakor & Alawiye, 1990; Ogbu, 1987, 1988, 1990; Samuda, 1975). Since environmental factors affect how a student performs in school programs, a logical extension is that the teacher's race has some influence on his or her styles, idiosyncrasies, perceptions, values, and orientation. The American Association of Colleges for Teacher Education (1987) reported that:

1. Blacks represent 16.2% of the children in public schools, but only 6.9% of the teachers.

2. Hispanics represent 9.1% of the children in public schools, but only 1.9% of the teachers.

3. Asian/Pacific Islanders represent 2.5% of the children in public schools, but only 0.9% of the teachers.

4. American Indians/Alaskan Natives represent 0.9% of the children in public schools, but only 0.6% of the teachers.

5. Whites represent 71.2% of the children in public schools, but 89.6% of the teachers. (p. 15)

As stated earlier, the General Education Initiative has the undergirding principle of *inclusiveness*. If this supposition is true, the issue of preparation of African Americans in teacher education programs should constitute a major part of any reform debates. The dearth of discussion on this issue emphasizes the tragedy facing African-American students in both general and special school programs.

Future Holds Promise

Davis (1990) explained that "the real value of the [General Education Initiative] debate lies in its potential to rigorously evaluate public education's commitment to serving at-risk students with a variety of special needs and disabilities" (p. 351). America's future is at stake when it addresses the complex educational problems confronting African Americans in school programs. An educational system in need of reform cannot afford to abdicate, abolish, or ignore movements such as the General Education Initiative or inclusion. Similarly, educators cannot continue to advocate, promise, or promote changes without encouraging discourse and making needed preparations. Kaufman and colleagues (1990) noted that "in the context of educational change, what passed as today's resolution may be tomorrow's problems" (p. 114). They acknowledged the impact of Public Law 94-142 in assuring a free, appropriate public education for all children, but submitted that children with disabilities "are not dropping out of special education, they are dropping out of school" (p. 109). Clearly, collaborative efforts between general and special educators are essential in meeting the broad educational reforms needed to ensure appropriate education for all students.

For some time, education has failed to meet the needs of many African Americans, and assignment to special education has led to labels and poor treatment of some students (Obiakor, 1992). Important questions remain when restructuring is proposed along dimensions related to the movement known as the General Education Initiative: Where do African Americans fit when the dual systems of general and special education are merged? Will the assessment instruments be restandardized, or will nontraditional assessment techniques be used? Will teachers and service providers undergo new sensitivity workshops on how to deal with African-American students in general and special education programs? What kind of curriculum will be used by teachers in a merged program?

These questions do not have easy answers. Jenkins, Pious, and Jewell were correct when they wrote, "It is unclear from the attention generated by the [General Education Initiative] that there is both large-scale agreement, that the way we educate low-achieving children is seriously flawed, and large-scale disagreement about how to make it better" (1990, p. 480).

Getting There from Here

Debate about ways to reform education will probably continue into the next century. The plight of African-American students in restructured general and special education programs cannot and should not be ignored in the midst of any discourse about partnerships in meeting the needs of student with disabilities. Contemporary practices will be continuously challenged to respond to the educational, social, economic, and cultural needs of *all* Americans. In addition, challenges to respond specifically to the issue of the overrepresentation of African Americans in special education programs will continue to be mounted. New and different programs such as the General Education Initiative and inclusionary practices have been advocated and designed to reach African-American students. The initiation of any reform program is never the problem; however, how individuals manage the program in individual classrooms represents a continuing challenge. Banks (1977) remarked that "We live in a world society beset with momentous social and human problems, many of which are related to ethnic hostility and conflict. Effective solutions to these problems can be found only by an active, compassionate, and ethnically sensitive citizenry capable of making sound decisions that will benefit our ethnically diverse world community" (p. 32).

What challenges face teachers when presenting information to African-American students in any kind of classroom? It is important that teachers foster a pluralistic society through multiethnic education in their classrooms (Banks, 1977, 1986; Gay, 1980). As a matter of common practice, teachers should acknowledge (a) the historical backgrounds of their African-American students, (b) the language and symbols that African-American students bring to class, (c) the behavioral patterns of African-American students, and (d) the events that have molded the African-American group members (Obiakor, 1992). Education should not be viewed simplistically as a white peoples' prerogative; it should be associated with democracy and real freedom for everyone. In making this connection, Marable (1990) raised the following question:

> If the curriculum of our public schools does not present the heritage, culture and history of African-Americans, if it ignores or downgrades our vital contributions for a more democratic society, our children are robbed of their heritage. They acquire a distorted perspective about ourselves and their communities. If they believe that African-American people have never achieved greatness, in the sciences, art, music, economics and the law, how can they excel or achieve for themselves? (p. 54)

In view of the problems confronting African-American students in school programs, it is unclear whether reform will ameliorate or worsen their plight. After all, had general educators done their job effectively, there would have been no special education. Lieberman (1990) asserted that "the true regular education initiative is P.L. 94-142 and least restrictive environment—public policy, opinion, and attitudes put the teeth in social legislation of this kind" (p. 561). Just as segregation of any students was not an acceptable answer, integration of all students may not be an appropriate answer. In fact, the best answer may simply not be known at this time. Algozzine and colleagues (1990) put it this way: "We are not convinced that the course of our field's condition is so promising that we can freely ignore any medicine, even those available without prescriptions that may not as yet be doctor-tested" (p. 556).

6

REFERENCES

Algozzine, B., Maheady, L., Sacca, K.C., O'Shea, L., & O'Shea, D. (1990). Sometimes patent medicine works: A reply to Braaten, Kauffman, Braaten, Polsgrove, and Nelson. *Exceptional Children, 56,* 552–557.

American Association of Colleges for Teacher Education. (1987). *Minority teacher recruitment and retention: A public policy issue.* Washington, DC: Author.

Anrig, G. R. (1985). Educational standards, testing, and equity. *Phi Delta Kappan, 66,* 623–625.

Banks, J. A. (1977). *Multiethnic education: Practices and promises.* Bloomington, IN: Phi Delta Kappa.

Banks, J. A. (1986, April). *Race, ethnicity, class, and education: A critical analysis of concepts and paradigms.* Paper presented at the Annual Meeting of the American Educational Research Association, San Francisco, CA.

Braaten, S., Kauffman, J. M., Braaten, B., Polsgrove, L., & Nelson, C. M. (1988). The regular education initiative: Patent medicine for behavioral disorders. *Exceptional Children, 55,* 21–28.

Byrnes, M. (1990). The regular education initiative debate: A view from the field. *Exceptional Children, 56,* 345–349.

Carnegie Forum on Education and the Economy. (1986). *A nation prepared: Teachers for the 21st century.* New York: Carnegie Foundation.

Corder, L. J., & Quisenberry, M. L. (1987). Early education and Afro-Americans: History, assumptions and implications for the future. *Early Education: Journal of the Association for Childhood Education International, 63*(3), 154–166.

Committee for Economic Development. (1985). *Investing in our children: Business and the public schools.* New York: Author.

Cuban, L. (1984). School reform by remote control: SR 813 in California. *Phi Delta Kappan, 66,* 213–215.

Cuban, L. (1990). Reforming again, again, and again. *Educational Researcher, 19*(1), 3–13.

Cummins, J. (1989). A theoretical framework for bilingual special education. *Exceptional Children, 56,* 111–119.

Davis, J. C., & Maheady, L. (1991). The regular education initiative: What do three groups of educational professionals think? *Teacher Education and Special Education, 14*(4), 211–220.

Davis, W. E. (1989). The regular education initiative debate: Its promises and problems. *Exceptional Children, 55,* 440–446.

Davis, W. E. (1990). Broad perspectives on the regular education initiative: Response to Byrnes. *Exceptional Children, 56,* 349–351.

Fuchs, D., & Fuchs, L. S. (1991). Framing the REI debate: Abolitionists vs. conservationists. In J. W. Lloyd, N. N. Singh, & A. C. Repp (Eds.), *The regular education initiative: Alternative perspectives on concepts, issues, and models* (pp. 241–255). Sycamore, IL: Sycamore.

Fuchs, D., Fuchs, L. S., Fernstrom, P., & Hohn, M. (1991). Toward a responsible reintegration of behaviorally disordered students. *Behavioral Disorders, 16,* 133–147.

Gay, G. (1980). Interactions in the culturally pluralistic classroom. In J. A. Banks (Ed.), *Education in the 80's: Multiethnic education.* Washington, DC: National Education Association.

Gould, S. J. (1981). *The mismeasure of man.* New York: Norton.

Hallenbeck, B. A., Kauffman, J. M., & Lloyd, J. W. (1993). When, how, and why educational decisions are made: Two case studies. *Journal of Emotional and Behavioral Disorders, 1,* 109–117.

Harvey, W. B., & Scott-Jones, D. (1985). We can't find any: The elusiveness of black faculty members in American higher education. *Issues in Education, 111*(1), 68–76.

Hilliard, A. G. (1975, July). *From aptitude treatment interaction toward creative mainstreaming: A response to Dr. Snow.* Paper presented at the U. S. Office of Education, BEH Leadership Training Institute, Minneapolis, MN.

Hilliard, A. G. (1989, December). Cultural style in teaching and learning. *The Education Digest,* pp. 20–23.

Holmes Group. (1988). From tomorrow's teachers. In K. Ryan & J. M. Cooper (Eds.), *Kaleidoscope: Readings in education* (5th ed.) (pp. 484–493). Boston: Houghton-Mifflin.

Jackson, J. L. (1988). In pursuit of equity, ethics, and excellence: The challenge to close the gap. In K. Ryan & J. M. Cooper (Eds.), *Kaleidoscope: Readings in education* (5th ed.) (pp. 444–448). Boston: Houghton-Mifflin.

Jenkins, J. R., Pious, C. G., & Jewell, M. (1990). Special education and the regular education initiative: Basic assumptions. *Exceptional Children, 56*, 479–491.

Kauffman, J., Gerber, M., & Semmel, M. (1988). Arguable assumptions underlying the regular education initiative. *Journal of Learning Disabilities, 21*, 6–12.

Kauffman, J. M., Cullinan, D., & Epstein, M. H. (1987). Characteristics of students placed in special education programs for the seriously emotionally disturbed. *Behavioral Disorders, 12*, 175–184.

Kauffman, J. M., & Lloyd, J. (1992). Restrictive educational placement of students with emotional and behavioral disorders: What we know and what we need to know. In R. B. Rutherford & S. R. Mather (Eds.), *Severe behavior disorders of children and youth* (Vol. 15, pp. 35–43). Reston, VA: Council for Children with Behavioral Disorders.

Kaufman, M. P., Kameenui, E. J., Birman, B. P., & Danielson, L. (1990). Special education and the process of change: Victim or master of educational reform? *Exceptional Children, 57,* 109–115.

Lauderdale, W. R. (1987). *Educational reform: The forgotten half.* Bloomington, IN: Phi Delta Kappa.

Lieberman, L. M. (1990). REI: Revisited . . . again. *Exceptional Children, 56*, 561–562.

Lilly, M. S. (1986). The relationship between general and special education: A new face on an old issue. *Counterpoint, 6*(1), 10.

Marable, M. (1990). Violence and crime in the black community: Part two of a two part series. *Jackson Advocate, 51*(19), 5A.

McKinney, J. D., & Hocutt, A. M. (1988). Policy issues in the evaluation of the regular education initiative. *Learning Disabilities Focus, 4*, 15–23.

Minton, H. L., & Schneider, F. W. (1980). *Differential psychology.* Prospect Heights, IL: Waveland.

National Commission on Excellence in Education. (1983). *A nation at risk: The imperative for educational reform.* Washington, DC: Author.

Obiakor, F. E. (1990, November). *Crisis in minority education.* Paper presented at the First National Social Science Association (NSSA) Conference, Washington, DC.

Obiakor, F. E. (1991, April). *African-American quandaries in school programs.* Paper presented at the General Meeting of the National Black Caucus of Special Educators, The Council for Exceptional Children, Atlanta, GA.

Obiakor, F. E. (1992). Embracing new special education strategies for African-American students. *Exceptional Children, 59*, 104–106.

Obiakor, F. E., & Alawiye, O. (1990, October). *Development of accurate self-concept in black children.* Paper presented at The Council for Exceptional Children Symposia on Culturally Diverse Exceptional Children, Albuquerque, NM.

Ogbu, J. U. (1987, March). *Types of cultural differences and minority school adjustment and performance.* Distinguished Visiting Professor Lecture Series No. 1, New Mexico State University, Las Cruces.

Ogbu, J. U. (1988). Human intelligence testing: A cultural ecological perspective. *National Forum: The Phi Kappa Phi Journal, 68*(2), 23–29.

Ogbu, J. U. (1990). Understanding diversity: Summary statements. *Education and Urban Society, 22*, 425–429.

Princes, C. W., & Obiakor, F. E. (1990). Disabled students: An area-specific model of self-concept. In J. J. Van Putten (Ed.), *Reaching new heights: Proceedings of the 1989 AHSSPPE conference* (pp. 35–50). Madison, WI: Omni.

Reynolds, M. C., Wang, M. C., & Walberg, H. J. (1987). The necessary restructuring of special and regular education. *Exceptional Children, 53,* 391–398.

Samuda, R. J. (1975). *Psychological testing of American minorities: Issues and consequences.* New York: Harper & Row.

Stainback, W., & Stainback, S. (1984). A rationale for the merger of special and regular education. *Exceptional Children, 51*, 102–111.

Stainback, W., & Stainback, S. (1991). A rationale for integration and restructuring: A synopsis. In J. W. Lloyd, N. N. Singh, & A. C. Repp (Eds.), *The regular education initiative: Alternative perspectives on concepts, issues, and models* (pp. 226–239). Sycamore, IL: Sycamore.

Staples, R. (1984), March/April). Racial ideology and intellectual racism: Blacks in academia. *The Black Scholar,* pp. 2–17.

Stedman, L. C. (1987). It's time we changed the effective schools formula. *Phi Delta Kappan, 69,* 215–224.

Walker, H. M., & Bullis, M. (1991). Behavior disorders and the social context of regular class integration: A conceptual dilemma? In J. W. Lloyd, N. N. Singh, & A. C. Repp (Eds.), *The regular education initiative: Alternative perspectives on concepts, issues, and models* (pp. 75–93). Sycamore, IL: Sycamore.

Will, M. (1986)). *Educating students with learning problems: A shared responsibility.* Washington, DC: U.S. Department of Education.

Ysseldyke, J. E., & Algozzine, B. (1990). *Introduction to special education* (2nd ed.). Boston: Houghton-Mif-flin.

Ysseldyke, J. E., Algozzine, B., & Thurlow, M. L. (1992). *Critical issues in special education* (2nd ed.). Boston: Houghton-Mifflin.

CHAPTER 2

Ecobehavioral Assessment: A New Methodology for Evaluating Instruction for Exceptional Culturally and Linguistically Diverse Students

Carmen Arreaga-Mayer
Judith J. Carta
Yolanda Tapia

The research literature in bilingual and regular education has devoted considerable attention to determining the effectiveness of procedures for educating students with limited English proficiency (LEP). While much of the research devoted to this topic involves examining whether instructional procedures were effective in meeting their goal (i.e., assisting children in acquiring educational and language skills), detailed objective data and instrumentation have most often focused on teacher or student behavior, rarely on the environment and least often on the interaction between the environment or ecology and behaviors (i.e., ecobehavioral assessment).

Bilingual education programs and special education programs share several important dimensions. Each field has received far too much empirically unsubstantiated criticism and far too little well-conceived or meaningful evaluation (Tymitz, 1983; Willig, 1981). Each field can also be characterized as controversial insofar as it has sought redress from documented inequities, from the courts and federal government as well as educational institutions (Cummins, 1983; Hakuta, 1985; Maheady, Towne, Algozzine, Mercer, & Ysseldyke, 1983; Ochoa, Pacheco, & Omark, 1983). In addition, both types of programs are exceedingly complex and call into question specific educational and social values in a way that other instructional program areas do not (Baca & Cervantes, 1984; Tymitz, 1983). In the field of bilingual education, the issue of the best type of services (maintenance versus transition), coupled with cultural pluralism, heterogeneous populations, exit-entry assessments, and the equal protection of the law, is often in conflict with intervention strategies, confounding the issue of what an ideal bilingual education program should be or accomplish. No one specific criterion is sufficient to measure and describe the variety of bilingual programs available, nor has any clearly defined variable emerged against which to evaluate the general adequacy or effectiveness of bilingual education (Ambert & Dew, 1983; Fradd & Hallman, 1983; Hakuta, 1985; O'Malley, 1978).

The evaluation of special education programs is no less complicated. The issues of referral, nondiscriminatory assessment, categorization and classification procedures, case conferences, mainstreaming, due process, parent involvement, staff training, and coordination of services all add to the difficulty of assessing program impact and effectiveness accurately (Baca & Bransford, 1982; Hakuta, 1985; Ortiz & Yates, 1983). Public Law 94-142, the Education for All Handicapped Children Act of 1975, with its mandates of individualized education programming and placement in less restrictive environments, has created added pressure for educators to develop effective instructional strategies and for administrators and researchers to develop evaluation strategies that facilitate statutory compliance but also make instructional sense.

The merging of the fields of bilingual education and special education into bilingual special education has presented program evaluators with even more methodological challenges and more demanding complications. Students in bilingual special education not only have limited English proficiency, they also experience specific learning problems and disabling conditions that interfere with the acquisition of English and retention of skills or content material (Baca & Cervantes, 1984; Tymitz, 1983). No categorical placements seem to fit the children with this double set of needs (Bernal, 1983; Cortes, 1977). Wolf (1978) stated that the conflict that currently besets the field of bilingual special education is exacerbated by evaluation efforts, particularly when those efforts rely on traditional outcome measures that in the past have not served either field well.

In summary, instructional strategies and programmatic issues have affected the direction, outcome, and validity of past evaluation studies in both bilingual and special education programs. Since bilingual special education programs are more than the sum of the two educational fields joined, these concerns affect the bilingual special education field with even greater intensity. Bernal (1983), in an essay discussing the trends in bilingual special education, emphasized that to establish the purview necessary for research, development, and evaluation agendas for bilingual special education, the following critical questions must be addressed:

1. What is the state of the art in bilingual special education in terms of educational intervention and basic research on program evaluation?

2. How much well-documented guidance can be given to practitioners in the field regarding essential features of intervention programs?

3. What are the research development and evaluation priorities affecting policy and accountability which could stem from inquiries into the essential features of intervention programs?

4. Which programs (e.g., bilingual, English as a Second Language [ESL], or English immersion special education programs) are most effective with different categories of children with disabilities who have limited English proficiency?

5. What are the long-term consequences of these interventions—cognitively, linguistically, educationally, and practically?

CURRENT BILINGUAL SPECIAL EDUCATION EFFICACY LITERATURE

Although some of the earliest studies reported negative outcomes of bilingual intervention programs (e.g., Baker & DeKanter, 1981; Danoff, Coles, McLaughlin, & Reynold, 1977a, 1977b, 1978a, 1978b), the most recently emerging body of longitudinal research indicates that bilingual intervention programs are successful in producing lasting gains in the academic and second language proficiency development of children in bilingual special education and mainstream placements (e.g., De La Garza & Medina, 1985; Medina, Saldate, & Mishra, 1985; Saldate, Mishra, & Medina, 1985; Willig, 1985). Although the consensus in the literature seems to be that these programs work, little attention has been focused on the following questions: (a) How do bilingual special education intervention programs work? (Ambert & Dew, 1983; Baca & Bransford, 1982); (b) For whom do they work? (Trueba, Guthrie & Au, 1981; Willig, 1985); and (c) Do some programs work better than others? (Arreaga-Mayer & Greenwood, 1986; Maheady, 1985; Tikunoff, 1983).

The answers to these questions become increasingly important as we strive to meet the needs of bilingual students receiving special education services in the face of cost-conscious state legislatures and the general public. Developers and administrators of bilingual special education programs need to know what the essential components of bilingual special education are and how they can improve upon those programs. In summary, now that we know that bilingual special education intervention works, we need to find out why it works.

At least two distinct yet intertwined reasons for conducting efficacy studies in bilingual special education exist: (1) to build the research base for promoting the development of more effective intervention models, and (2) to justify support for continuing and expanding services to bilingual children with disabilities and their families (Maheady, 1985). The first reason, which will be called the *instructional perspective,* is directed at program developers, service providers, parents, and researchers—those individuals who are most interested in the issue of whether interventions bring about changes in bilingual children's growth and development. Studies of this type are primarily concerned with two types of outcome measures: (1) school-related variables such as achievement measures, retention in grade, and special class placement and (2) long-range outcomes such as employment, social competence, and general adjustment in later life. The alternative perspective on efficacy studies, called the *accountability perspective,* is directed at legislators, school superintendents, and agency directors, individuals who know little about intervention but who nonetheless want to ensure that funds allocated for these programs get the "biggest bang for the bucks." What is lacking is an *ecobehavioral perspective* that focuses on both program accountability (does the program work?) and program efficiency (does the program work in the best possible way at current funding levels?).

At present, studies related to the efficacy of bilingual intervention focus almost exclusively on the first question. A number of different program outcomes for bilingual students with disabilities have been used in these evaluations. A recent computer search of the Educational Resources Information Center (ERIC) and the National Clearinghouse for Bilingual Education (NCBE) data bases for reports on the effectiveness of bilingual special education revealed 108 citations. The outcomes of these studies are presented in Table 2-1. The literature clearly reveals numerous evaluation studies from the instructional perspective, but a dearth of evaluation reports derived from the accountability perspective. If policy makers are to be convinced that

TABLE 2-1

Outcome Measures Employed in Past Efficacy Research on Bilingual Special Education

Outcome Measures	Percent of Studies Employing Measures (n = 108)
Gains in second language acquisition	26
Improvement in achievement scores while enrolled in bilingual program	19
Gains in curriculum related tests of development	10
Improvement in behavioral adjustment, self-concept, or social interaction	9
Educational placement on leaving the program	9
Teacher's ratings of program graduate's behaviors	5
Cost effectiveness of program	5
Improvement in IQ scores	3

Other, less frequently mentioned types of outcomes included:

— Percentage of pupils retained in grades after placement in regular elementary grade classes

— Amount of parental involvement in the program

bilingual intervention is effective, instructional research needs to be taken one step further. We need to bridge the gap between the instructional question, "Does it work?" and the accountability question, "How well does it work?" by answering the ecobehavioral question, "What makes it work?" We need to examine programmatic factors responsible for the encouraging outcomes that bilingual special education intervention has produced.

Problems with Current Evaluation Research

The review of literature on effectiveness of bilingual programs revealed eight categories of outcome measures used to evaluate program effectiveness. While these measures have been practical in documenting that students with disabilities who have limited English proficiency have made important gains while participating in bilingual special education programs, they have provided little information about why those changes have occurred. This is because in most evaluation studies, little, if any, attention has been paid to measuring the independent variable, the bilingual special education treatment. Past evaluation studies have treated bilingual interventions as unitary variables that were either present or not present. Rarely have the many components that differentiate one program from another been measured, such as the behaviors engaged in by the teacher and the student, the objectives taught, and the implementation of instructional procedures.

The science of bilingual special education service delivery can move forward only when successful programs can be replicated, and this can happen only when the independent variable, the bilingual special education intervention, has been clearly delineated, assessed, and empirically examined. What is needed are evaluations directed at including answers to the more challenging questions: What works in the program? Why is it working? What is not working, and how can those who implement the program make it work better? Answers to these questions require more than a traditional outcomes-only approach to assessment. They require the use of evaluation strategies that are responsive to the complexities of individual children, individual programs, and individual contexts.

Ecobehavioral Assessment and Analysis: A Technology for Measuring Classroom Processes

Ecobehavioral analysis has recently received attention as a sophisticated and applicable methodology for studying educational settings. Ecobehavioral analysis is defined as:

> a means of assessing program variables through systematic observation and measuring the moment by moment effects of an array of variables upon student behavior. The momentary interactions between immediate program variables as ecological stimuli and student behaviors are the units of analysis for predicting or otherwise investigating program outcomes such as developmental gain or long term achievement. (Carta & Greenwood, 1985, p. 92).

The ecobehavioral approach to assessment emerged from a combination of three different theoretical fields: *ecological psychology* and its concerns with assessment of aspects of the environment within strategies for observational measurements (Barker & Wright, 1968; Bronfenbrenner, 1979), the designs of *applied behavior analysis* (Baer, Wolf, & Risley, 1987; Bijou, Patterson, & Ault, 1968; Rogers-Warren & Warren, 1977), and the *process-product research* in education (Brophy & Good, 1986; Dunkin & Biddle, 1974). Thus, the ecobehavioral approach goes beyond the input (independent variable–intervention)–output (dependent variable–outcome measure) strategy of assessment by providing for the assessment of ongoing, moment-to-moment processes that affect students. This approach provides an advancement in current assessment technology in that it allows us to measure and define the specifics of learning events as they occur and how subsequent student responses change and interact in a sequential fashion (Greenwood,

Carta, & Atwater, 1991). Thus, while the ecobehavioral approach equips us with a more precise and systematic means of ensuring program effectiveness, fidelity, and replication, this approach has yet to be applied to bilingual special education programs. Our technology of assessment in bilingual education remains focused primarily on students' behavior and has yet to provide quantitative assessments of students' performance as interactions within their learning environments.

In the past few years, researchers have advanced the use of ecobehavioral analysis in evaluating the effectiveness of instruction and interventions in a variety of educational settings. Work in ecobehavioral methodology at the Juniper Gardens Children's Project has resulted in development of several comprehensive observation systems (Greenwood, Carta, Kamps, & Arreaga- Mayer, 1990). This technology has taken on greater applied significance in the evaluation of instructional interventions. For example, the Code for Instructional Structure and Student Academic Response (CISSAR) (Stanley & Greenwood, 1983) makes it possible to record 53 separate variables classified into 6 major categories: activities (subject of instruction), curriculum task type, structure of instructional group, teacher position with respect to target student, teacher behavior, and student behavior. The code is described as an ecobehavioral observation system because it yields scores relating ecological (input and process) variables to student behavior. The code was designed to sample sequentially the ecology of instruction (activity, tasks, structure, teacher position, and teacher behavior) and the student behavior that ensues. This sequential sampling allows for systematic analyses of the interactions between ecological and student behavioral variables across time.

Analysis of Ecobehavioral Processes

Ecobehavioral analysis can be used to describe observations of specific variables in which the frequency of each coded event can be totaled and expressed in terms of the grand total of all the coded events, as a percentage score or an unconditional proportion. These *molar* descriptions are proportions or session estimates of the relative rates of occurrence of each coded classroom event. In addition, classroom events that occur contiguously (co-occurring in the same time interval or following each other in subsequent intervals) can be combined to form conditional proportion scores. Summaries of these jointly occurring events can then be combined to form *molecular* descriptions, the conditional relationship between ecology and behavioral events. These molecular descriptions are conditional probability statements regarding the likelihood that two or more events (ecological and behavioral) will occur simultaneously in close sequential time intervals. In ecobehavioral analysis, the classroom processes defined using molar and molecular descriptions achieve added significance when they are related to product measures (i.e., language or achievement gains), that is, *product-process* analyses of achievement gains.

Greenwood, Delquadri, and Hall (1984) demonstrated the utility of ecobehavioral data using molar CISSAR results to contrast instruction within inner-city and suburban schools. For example, fourth-grade teachers in inner-city schools were found to use different instructional tasks than teachers in suburban schools. In inner-city schools, fourth-grade teachers were more likely to use audiovisual media (overhead projectors, films, etc.). In suburban schools, teachers were more likely to assign seatwork and allow students to work independently. When the behaviors of students in these groups were compared, inner-city students were found to exhibit significantly lower levels of academic responding than suburban students, even when IQ and social economic status were statistically controlled (Greenwood et al., 1981). Ysseldyke, Thurlow, Mecklenburg, Graden, and Algozzine (1984) used molar CISSAR results to examine differences in service delivery models for students with learning disabilities. They found that these students exhibited levels of active academic responding when placed in regular classes that were similar to the levels they exhibited in special education classes. These differential findings are molar descriptions of classroom ecology and student behavior that are helpful in making global comparisons between programs or educational settings.

Molecular CISSAR descriptions of classrooms have revealed the diversity of momentary ecological stimulus arrangements that students experience within single lessons and the variability in specific academic behaviors temporally associated with each particular arrangement of classroom ecological variables. Carta, Greenwood, and Robinson (1987), using an ecobehavioral system of observations within early intervention programs for children with disabilities, reported that play, as an activity, occurred as frequently as preacademics (21% vs. 24% of the day, respectively). Student behaviors during these activities were also widely different. For example, "attend" (47%) was the most frequent behavior during preacademics while "manipulate" (32%) was predominant during play. These molecular descriptions of co-occurring classroom events and related student responses are important in designing and replicating effective interventions.

Process-product analyses using the CISSAR have been used to find the relationships of classroom or student response variables to student achievement. Greenwood, Delquadri, and Hall (1984) reported that a composite of seven student behavior variables termed *Academic Responding* (writing, academic game playing, reading aloud, reading silently, engaging in academic discussion, answering an academic question, and asking an academic question) was most predictive of achievement ($r = .42$). The individual behaviors of writing and silent reading were also significantly correlated to student achievement. Attentive behavior, defined as looking at the teacher, the lesson, or a peer answering a question, was not a significant correlate of achievement.

Thurlow, Ysseldyke, Graden, and Algozzine (1984) used the CISSAR code to contrast five levels of learning disability (LD) service delivery models. Observational data on 26 students for 2 entire school days revealed some differences in classroom ecological variables. In general, students in settings receiving more specialized help were allocated less time for academic activities and for entire group teaching structures than were students in less restrictive settings. On the other hand, students in the more restrictive settings were allocated more time in individual teaching structures. When relationships between molar descriptions of variables and student achievement gains were explored, a positive relationship between academic responding variables and achievement was found as well as a corresponding negative relationship between other competing inappropriate behaviors and academic achievement. Thus, through an ecobehavioral approach the researchers were able to define the ways classroom variables affect student behaviors and, subsequently, student achievement.

Although it has been demonstrated that an ecobehavioral approach can ascertain the specific elements of programmatic success at the elementary grade level for monolingual students, the need for making similar determinations for bilingual students with limited English proficiency remains. Once researchers, program developers, administrators, and teachers in bilingual intervention programs have a knowledge base concerning the variables responsible for the success of bilingual special education programs, they are more likely to replicate and expand upon these successes. The first step is the development of an appropriate assessment device that provides information about the instructional interactions that occur in classrooms for bilingual students with disabilities. In order to provide this type of critical information about the bilingual special education settings, the instrument must be complex enough to capture the sequence of teacher behaviors and student responses and elements of the bilingual special education classroom ecology.

A PROTOTYPE ECOBEHAVIORAL APPROACH

A sample prototype observational code developed by the authors appears in Table 2-2. An expanded version of this instrument, the Ecobehavioral System for the Contextual Recording of Interactional Bilingual Environments (ESCRIBE), can be used to assess ecobehavioral processes for a single student observed during individual sessions or spanning an entire school day, in special and/or mainstreamed settings. Student observations can then be summarized to provide the following types of descriptions of classrooms serving students with limited English proficiency:

TABLE 2-2

ESCRIBE: Categories, Codes, Descriptions, and Examples

Categories	Number of Codes	Description	Examples of Codes
Ecological			
Setting	11	Service delivery setting	Regular Class, Resource Room, Therapy Room, Library, Computer Lab
Instructional model	7	Instruction delivery model	Native Language Instruction, Full Bilingualism, English Immersion
Activity	17	Subject of instruction	Reading, Math, Language, Spelling
Materials	8	Curriculum materials	Books, Worksheets, Manipulatives
Language of materials	5	Language of curriculum materials used	English, Not English, Mixed, No Language
Instructional grouping	5	Instructional patterns	Whole-class Instruction, Small-Group Instruction, One-to-one Instruction, Independent Work
Teacher			
Teacher definition	8	Person teaching target student	Regular, Special, or Language Education Teachers, Aide, Peer
Teacher focus	4	To whom teacher behavior is directed	Target Student Only, Target Student and Others, None
Teacher language	5	Oral or written language used	English, Not English, Mixed, No Language
Teacher corrections/ affirmations	3	Quality of teacher's statements	Corrections, Affirmations, Neither
Teacher behavior	12	Teacher's behavior relative to target student	Questions-, Command- or Talk-Academic, Talk-Nonacademic, Praise/Approval, Nonverbal Prompt
Student			
Language initiating/ responding behavior	3	Classfies student's oral or written descriptions	Self-initiated Response to a Teacher's Behavior, Neither
Oral responses	5	Description of verbal behavior as it relates to academic activity	Talk Academic, Talk Management, Talk Social
Student language	5	Desciption of oral or written language used by student	English, Not English, Mixed, No Language
Activity-related behavior	11	Behavior or responses made directly to an academic activity	Writing, Reading Aloud, Talking

1. Molar descriptions of programs serving learners with disabilities who have limited English proficiency, derived by computing the percentage occurrence of each variable on the code, provide statements about the different classroom ecologies, such as the percentage of the school day spent in specific language acquisition activities and what type of instructional model, grouping, and language usage occurred during each activity. Similar descriptions can be made about the proportion of the day that the teacher engaged in various behaviors or languages and the types of behaviors and languages the student emitted.

2. Molecular descriptions of programs derived by computing conditional probabilities of various combinations of variables on the code will enable the researcher to answer the following types of questions: Given a specific instructional delivery model or instructional grouping, in what types of behaviors and language is the teacher most likely to be engaged? Given a specific type of activity or materials, in what types of behavior is the student most likely to be engaged? Given a specific teacher behavior and language of instruction, in what types of behavior and language usage is the student most likely to be engaged?

3. Process-product analyses are conducted by correlating specific ecobehavioral processes with outcome measures such as gain scores on language acquisition and dominance tests, measures of academic achievement, or measures of successful transitions to regular or mainstreamed environments.

These three types of descriptions can be used in several ways to evaluate intervention programs for students with disabilities in regular and or special education settings who have limited English proficiency. First, they can provide the basis for the definition of program variables across different types of instructional models in a quantifiable manner. For example, settings exemplifying different instructional delivery models (e.g., native language instruction, full bilingualism, or English immersion) can be described qualitatively and empirically and contrasted across variables such as activities, materials, language, and behaviors engaged in by teachers and students. Following the same pattern, programs that reflect different service delivery models can be equated—for example mainstreamed versus self-contained or half-day versus full-day programs.

Second, molar and molecular descriptions can be used to evaluate the fidelity of program replications. If an original program model can be described quantifiably across a variety of dimensions such as content taught, the materials and language used, specific teacher behaviors, and so forth, then these can become a template against which replications can be measured and compared.

Third, molar and molecular descriptions can provide a means for documenting specific changes and variations in programs—for example, changes incurred by the institution of a new curriculum, such as presentation format or instructional language. If ecobehavioral observations are recorded before and after the curriculum changes, molar and molecular descriptions derived from observational records can be analyzed in a time series fashion. Such analysis can document shifts in the specific independent variable being manipulated (e.g., activity, materials, teacher behaviors). Similarly, occurrences of student behavior with the curriculum variations can be monitored.

Fourth, process-product analyses using molar descriptions of student behaviors can be used to determine the specific classroom behaviors that are most related to language and academic gains. This type of evaluation will equip the field of bilingual special education with the information needed to determine the skills that are most predictive of language and academic gains. This type of information will assist program developers in selecting behaviors that will be the focus of the intervention program.

Fifth, the molecular descriptions of ecobehavioral interactions can be used for prescriptive teaching. That is, they can be used to make determinations of the specific combinations of ecological and teacher variables that are most related to the skills needed in the classroom and are critical to the acquisition or maintenance of language and academic achievement. These language or instructional variables can then become the targets for improvement.

PILOT STUDY

During the 1991–1992 school year, we conducted a pilot study in which the ESCRIBE system was used to assess the classroom instruction provided for students with limited English proficiency who were identified as receiving special education services or being at risk for developmental disabilities. This study provided a rich description of potentially influential programmatic and linguistic variables and their subsequent behavioral impact.

For this pilot study, data were collected on 111 variables across 36 students within 4 elementary-level school settings and 26 different classrooms. The instructional models represented in the sample included English immersion, full bilingualism, special education, bilingual special education, and English as a second language (ESL). The participants (N = 36) were observed for 6 full school days each for a total of 213 days and 1,491 hours. When the various combinations of variables and the different levels of analysis previously discussed were studied, the array of results available for interpretation was enormous. For the purpose of this chapter, we have chosen to focus on the results that illustrate the types of analyses available through the ecobehavioral approach to assessment.

RESULTS

Molar Descriptions

The first analyses were based on the combined data set, including all 213 days of observations across the 4 schools and 26 classrooms. These data allowed global descriptions to be made regarding ecobehavioral events on a typical classroom day for this population, based on our sample of 36 students. The first analysis addressed the question of time devoted to instructional activities. The data in Figure 2-1 show that the most frequently occurring activity was math at 20%. The next most frequently occurring activities were reading at 18%, language arts at 16%, social studies and science at 7%, and spelling and transition at 5%, with all other activities occurring less than 5% of the time. These data portray an emphasis on academic skills with these students.

The data presented in Figure 2-2 addressed the question of typical teacher behavior. The most frequently occurring teacher behavior was "Talk Academic" at 28%. "Teacher Attention" (i.e., looking at student/students or at the students' instructional or play materials) occurred 19% of the time, and "No Response" (i.e., no attending to student/students or their materials) occurred 15% of the time. Use of "Command Academic," "Question Academic," and "Talk Nonacademic" behaviors occurred with equal frequency (8–9%). These data revealed that the "Teacher Attention" and "No Response" behaviors, both eliciting less active academic and linguistic engagement from students, were more predominant in a typical school day than "Question" and "Command Academic" behaviors, both identified as highly academic- and language-engaging behaviors (see Figure 2-2).

A third analysis addressed the language used during instruction. Figure 2-3 shows that English was the most frequently used language of instruction at 58%. "Not English" (i.e., Spanish) was used only 5% of the time, and "No Language" (i.e., no verbal or written language) was coded at a frequency of 37% of the instructional time. These data depict an emphasis on the use of English or "No Language" (i.e., verbal or written) for the instruction of students with limited English proficiency who had disabilities or were developmentally at risk.

The fourth level of analysis addressed the question of student behaviors. Figure 2-4 depicts the students' language-related behaviors. The data revealed that the most frequently coded behaviors were the students' use of "No Language" and "No Talk," both at 92%. The students used English 8% of the time and "Not English" (i.e., Spanish) only 1% of the time. The students were engaged in "Academic Talk" only 5% of the time, the highest frequency of oral responses

FIGURE 2-1

Average Occurrence of Activities

Typical Classroom Day
General Molar Description

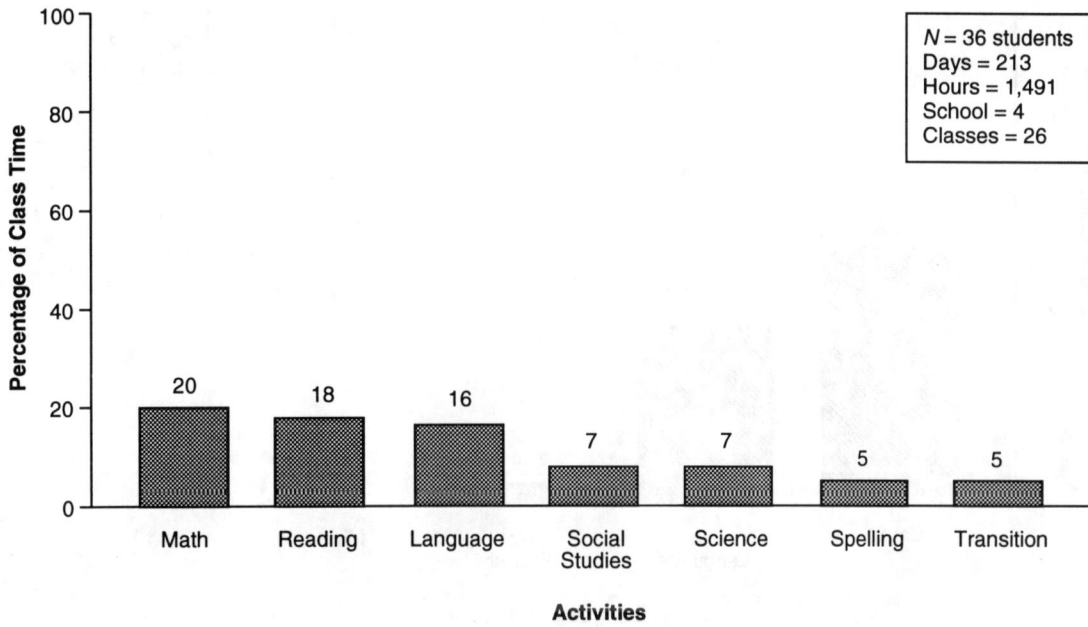

N = 36 students
Days = 213
Hours = 1,491
School = 4
Classes = 26

FIGURE 2-2

Average Occurrence of Teacher Behaviors

Typical Classroom Day
General Molar Description

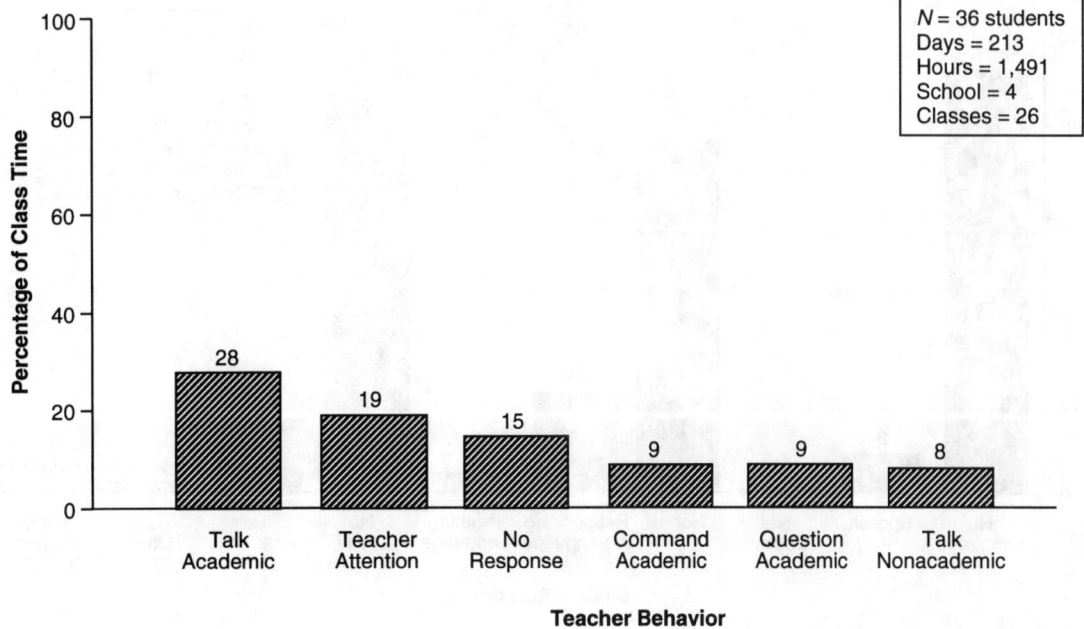

N = 36 students
Days = 213
Hours = 1,491
School = 4
Classes = 26

FIGURE 2-3

Average Occurrence of Language Instruction

Typical Classroom Day
General Molar Description

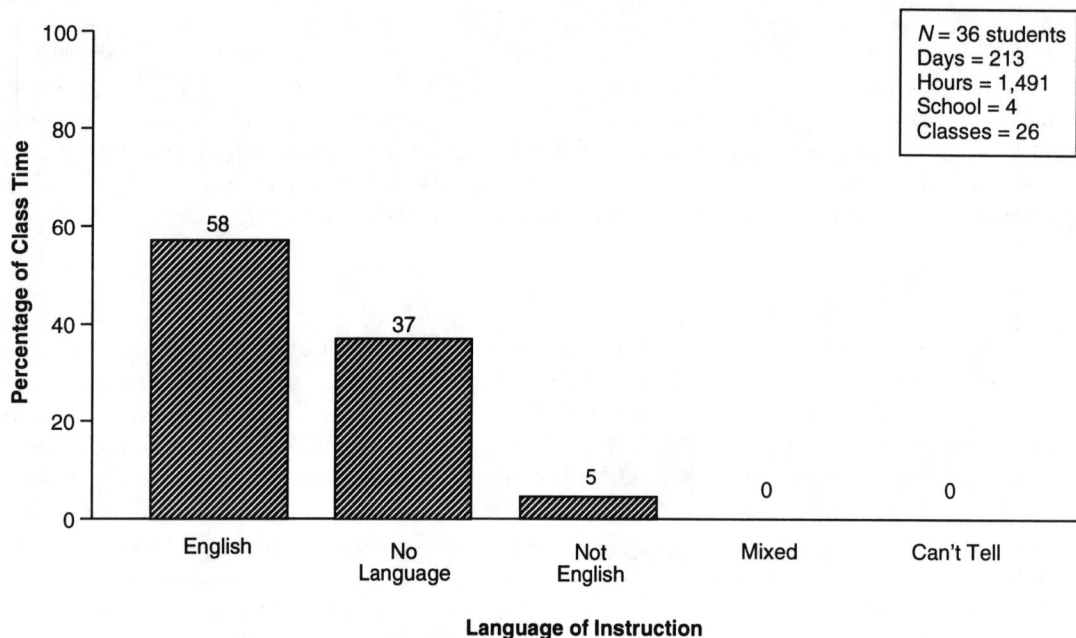

N = 36 students
Days = 213
Hours = 1,491
School = 4
Classes = 26

Language of Instruction

FIGURE 2-4

Average Occurrence of Student Language Response

Typical Classroom Day
General Molar Description

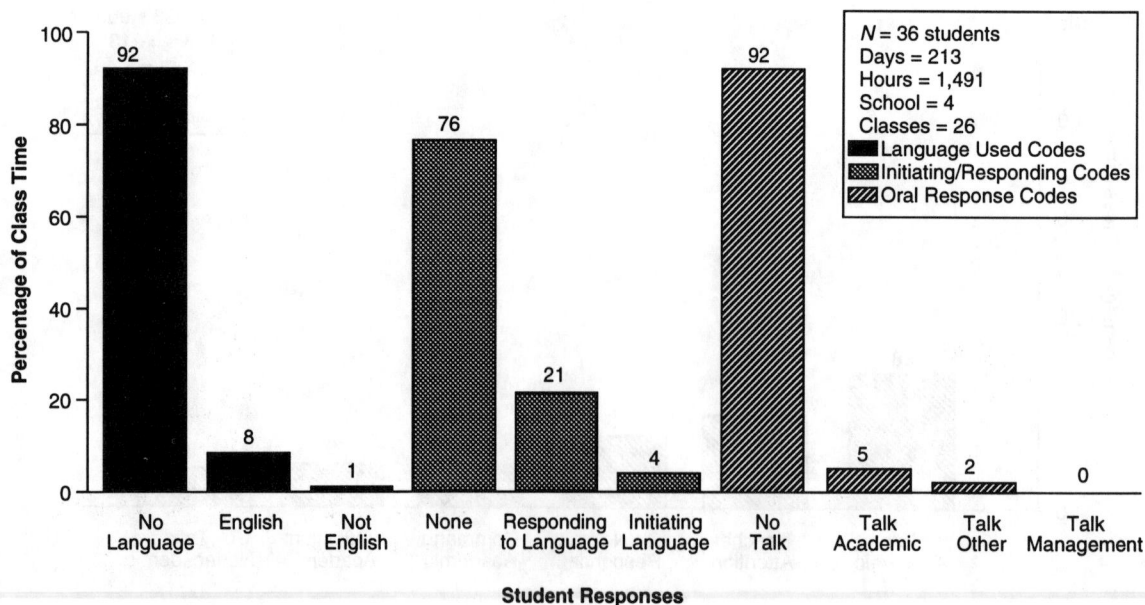

N = 36 students
Days = 213
Hours = 1,491
School = 4
Classes = 26
■ Language Used Codes
▦ Initiating/Responding Codes
▨ Oral Response Codes

Student Responses

coded, followed by 2% of the time engaged in "Other Talk" (i.e., social). The students spent 76% of the day neither initiating nor responding to language (verbal or written); 21% responding to language initiated by another adult, peer, or instructional material; and only 4% initiating language. These data are extremely informative as to the quality of linguistic opportunities that students with limited English proficiency receive during a typical academic day. If these students are to increase their use of and fluency in English and/or maintain their native languages, the frequency and quality of their language behaviors need to change.

Figure 2-5 addresses the occurrence of student activity-related behaviors. The data indicate that the most frequently coded behavior was attending (i.e., looking at a teacher who was instructing or discussing, or at a peer involved in an interaction with the target, or at some instructional material), occurring in 38% of all intervals. The total active engagement of students in academic behaviors (44%) was slightly less than half of the school day, while the active engagement of students in oral language responses occurred only 7% of the total school day.

School Comparisons

While the data presented provided an overall picture of the typical day for students with limited English proficiency who have disabilities or are developmentally at risk, the analyses that follow sampled another molar comparison capability of the ESCRIBE system: school comparisons. These analyses can refine global data by examining effects within and across specific schools and or service delivery models. For the purpose of this chapter, school comparisons based on the category of "Student Activity-Related Responses" (representing 11 codes out of 111 total codes) will be illustrated. Schools 1 and 3 were traditional English immersion schools with pull-out special education, bilingual special education, and ESL services. School 2 was a mathematics, science, and language magnet school with special services provided through instructional labs, special education, bilingual special education, and ESL services. School 4 was a Spanish language

FIGURE 2-5

Average Occurrence of Student Behavior

Typical Classroom Day
General Molar Description

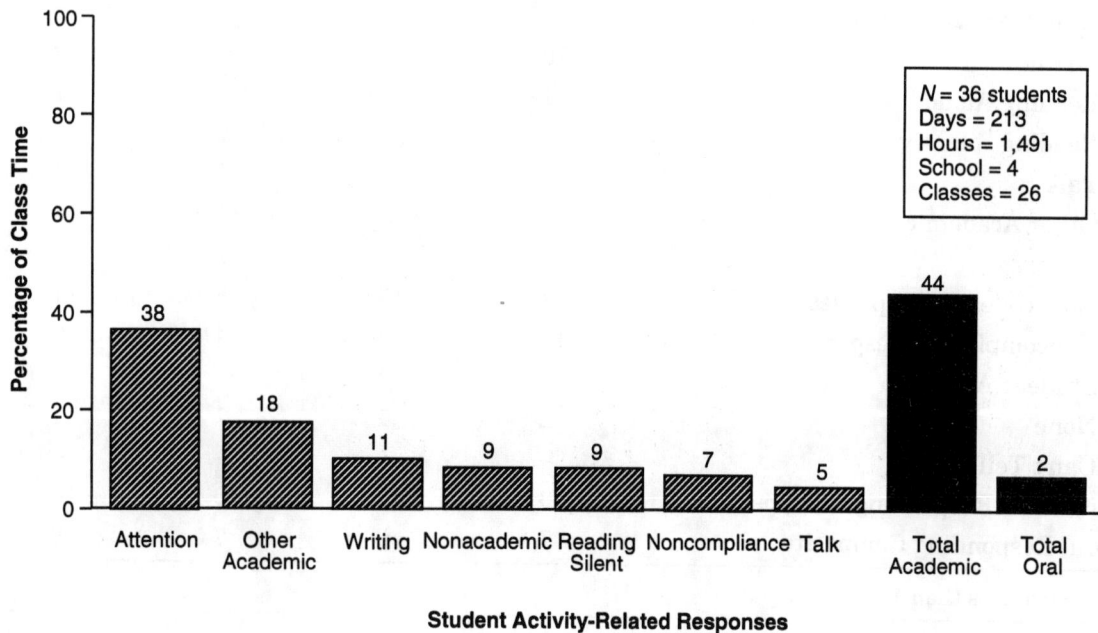

Student Activity-Related Responses

21

magnet school providing full bilingual instruction, special education, bilingual special education, language labs, and ESL services.

The individual school analyses provide an in-depth look into variables affecting academic and linguistic achievement and provide descriptive analyses of school events. For example, regardless of the type of instructional models represented in all the schools (see Table 2-3), slight variations occurred in the frequency of total active engagement in academic responding (range 40–50%) and oral responding (range 6–8%). The largest discrepancy sampled by this category occurred in the "Noncompliance" subcategory, which averaged 7% overall and ranged from 4% to 15% across schools.

School comparisons such as these help refine our research hypotheses concerning the problem of low student engagement and the configuration of the school or classroom environment in terms of ecological and teacher behavior as they affect student academic and language responses.

Comparisons Within Classrooms

The next analysis addressed the question of student variation within a classroom in response to the instructional programs. The data for three target students in Classroom 9 (School 4: full bilingualism instructional model) are presented in Table 2-4 with regard to teacher behavior and language of instruction. All students were identified as being at risk for disabilities and all participated in full bilingualism, language labs, and ESL instructional programs. Each student was observed for 6 days. While many similarities were noted, other interesting differences existed among these students served in the same learning environments.

The most frequently occurring teacher behavior for Sancho and Angel was "Talk Academic" (22%, 30%). Herman's highest frequency of teacher behavior was in the "No Response" subcate-

TABLE 2-3

School Comparison Summary from ESCRIBE Observations

	School			
ESCRIBE Code	1	2	3	4
Student Activity-Related Responses				
Writing	10	12	12	9
Reading Aloud	1	1	1	1
Reading Silently	7	10	12	7
Talk	6	5	5	6
Other Academic	16	18	19	16
Exercise	–*	–	1	1
Nonacademic Responses	7	10	8	11
Noncompliance Responses	15	6	4	6
Student Attention	36	37	37	41
None	2	1	1	1
Can't Tell	–	–	–.	–
Academic Responding Composite	40	45	50	40
Oral Responding Composite	7	6	7	8

* – = 0 or less than 1%

TABLE 2-4

**Comparison of Students in Classroom 9 Across Teacher Behavior
and Language of Instruction: Percent Occurrences**

	Student		
Category	Herman	Sancho	Angel
Teacher Behavior			
Question Academic	8	8	11
Command Academic	9	11	10
Talk Academic	21	22	30
Talk Nonacademic	9	9	10
Nonverbal Prompt	7	5	3
Teacher Attention	17	19	18
Praise/Approval	1	2	1
Disapproval	3	4	2
Read Aloud	2	3	2
Sing	0	1	1
No Response	23	16	12
Language of Instruction			
English	37	47	46
Not English	17	12	21
Mixed	0	0	0
No Language	46	40	32
Can't Tell	0	1	1

gory (i.e., no teacher attention or interaction) at 23%, yet "Talk Academic" also occurred at a fairly high level for this student (21%). All three students received similar-frequency occurrences of "Teacher Attention" behavior.

The most frequently occurring language of instruction for Sancho and Angel was English (47%, 46%) while Herman received only 37%. Herman received the highest frequency of occurrence in "No Language" (i.e., no verbal or written language) at 46%, yet Sancho and Angel also received fairly high levels of "No Language" teacher behavior (40%, 32%). The use of "Not English" (i.e, Spanish) for instruction, however, varied widely across subjects at 17%, 12%, and 21% respectively (see Table 2-4).

These results demonstrated that the teacher behaviors and languages used for instruction can show consistency in their structure but can also depict student differences in magnitude of specific variables.

Descriptions of Individual Students' Daily Variations

The two panels in Figure 2-6 illustrate the relative magnitude of one student's percentage scores for two subcategories of student activity responses (upper panel) and total academic and oral responding (lower panel) while receiving services in a special education resource classroom. These

FIGURE 2-6

**Range of Occurrence Across Days for One Student
in Resource Room: Special Education**

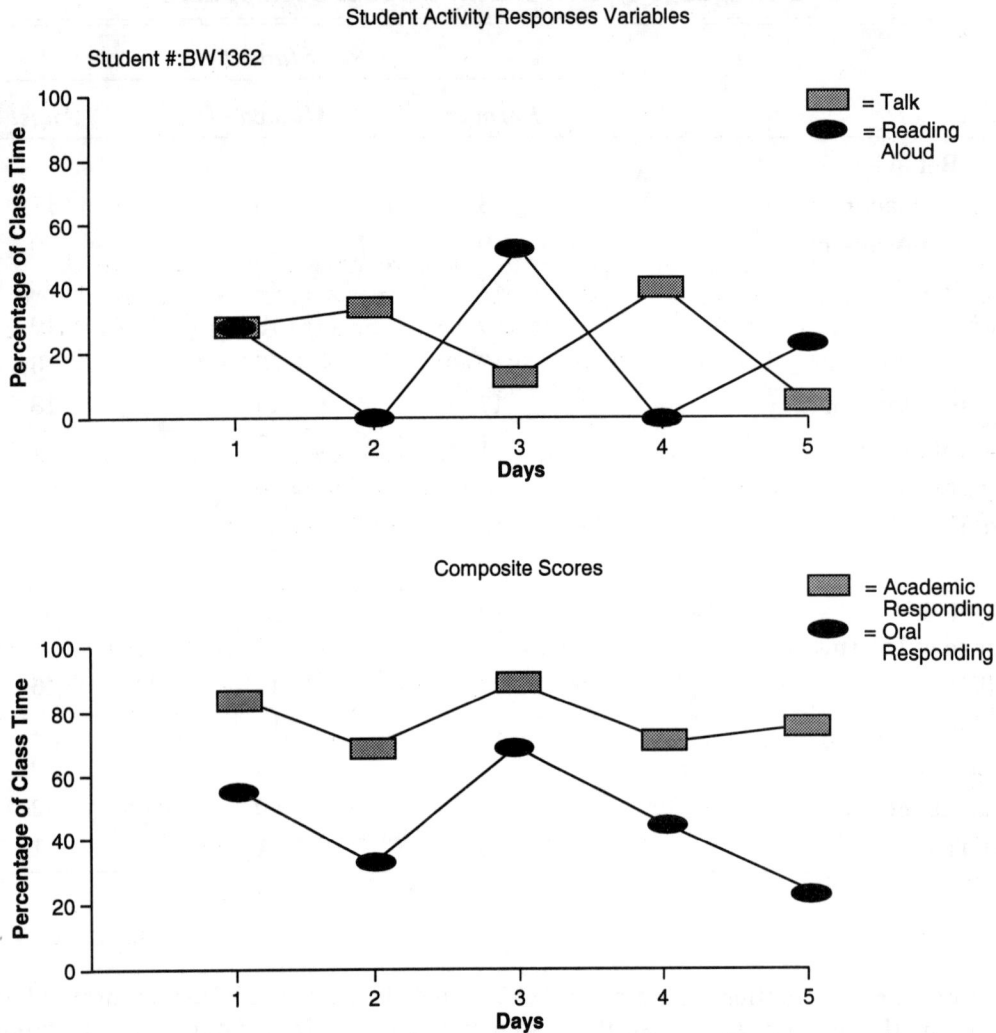

Student Activity Responses Variables

Composite Scores

data not only depict daily variations, they were selected to illustrate the relative range in magnitudes within subcategory codes.

The upper panel illustrates the daily differences in the student responses of "Talk" and "Reading Aloud" during special education resource room services. "Talk" was the most frequently occurring activity response and ranged from 14% to 39% (average of 24%) over the 5 days sampled. "Reading Aloud" occurred less frequently than "Talk" and ranged from 0 to 52% (average of 19%). The behaviors exhibited great variability with alternating days of higher frequency, with the exception of Day 1, when both behaviors occurred with the same frequency (28%).

The lower panel depicts the overall variations of the composite scores for academic and oral responding (active engagement scores). Academic responding averaged 76% over the 5 days sampled (range 67%–89%), while oral responding averaged 43% (range 23%–33%). The student's overall active engagement while participating in special education services was higher for academic and oral responding than his overall typical day, with academic responding at 45% (range 31–57%) and oral responding at 12% (range 8–17%).

Summary of Molar Analyses

These analyses are useful in providing general descriptions about the structure of time spent within different ecological variables (e.g., different instructional models, different activities, materials, language usage, grouping configurations, service delivery models), and within various teacher and student behaviors. Molar analyses, as illustrated in the data, can be useful in making comparisons across settings, students, and days for individual students. Collectively, these particular data confirm an important point, that bilingual intervention is not a unitary variable that is either present or not present, but rather a multitude of variables of different strength.

Molecular Descriptions

Molecular analyses were conducted to determine the influences of ecological or teacher behavior variables on students' behavior or language usage from a temporal correlational and causal perspective. Table 2-5 presents one such analysis based upon the consolidation of 6 full days of observation for one student. This student's teachers were concerned about the frequency and quality of his oral language usage during the school day.

The molecular descriptions based on the conditional probability analysis of the student's oral responses by instructional setting revealed important temporal correlations. The highest frequency of "Talk" occurred while the student was in the regular classroom. However, the student spent the highest percentage of time engaged in "Talk Academic" while participating in special education. During bilingual special education the student spent 100% of his talk behavior engaged in "Talk Academic," and 94% while in English-only special education. The student spent 87% of his talk behavior in "Talk Academic" during ESL services, 63% during library, and 51% during regular classroom services. In contrast, the student spent the highest percentage of time engaged in "Talk Other" (i.e., social) while in the regular classroom and the lowest while receiving special education services. These differences suggest the need to examine additional ecological factors across these settings in order to further isolate the elements or techniques accelerating oral language usage.

A second sample of molecular analysis addressed the causal relationship between active engagement in academic/language use behaviors (academic responding/oral responding) and instructional grouping (whole class/small group). As presented in Figure 2-7, the highest frequency of active academic responding occurred during the small-group instruction format; however, the frequency of oral responding did not demonstrate similar causal effects. Small-group

TABLE 2-5

Conditional Probability Analysis: Oral Responses ↔ Setting + Talk

	RC T	SP T	RR T	LY T	THR T
TA	0.514	0.943	0.870	0.636	1.000
TM	0.143			0.091	
TO	0.329	0.029	0.130	0.273	
NT	0.014	0.029			

Type of Talk: TA = Talk Academic, TM = Talk Management, TO = Talk Other, NT = No Talk
Setting: RC = Regular Classroom (Full Bilingualism), SP = Special Education, RR = Resource
Room-ESL, LY = Library
THR = Therapy-Bilingual Special Education, T = Talk.

FIGURE 2-7

Causal Relationship Between Active Engagement and Instructional Grouping

Comparison of Academic and Oral Responding
as a Function of Instructional Grouping

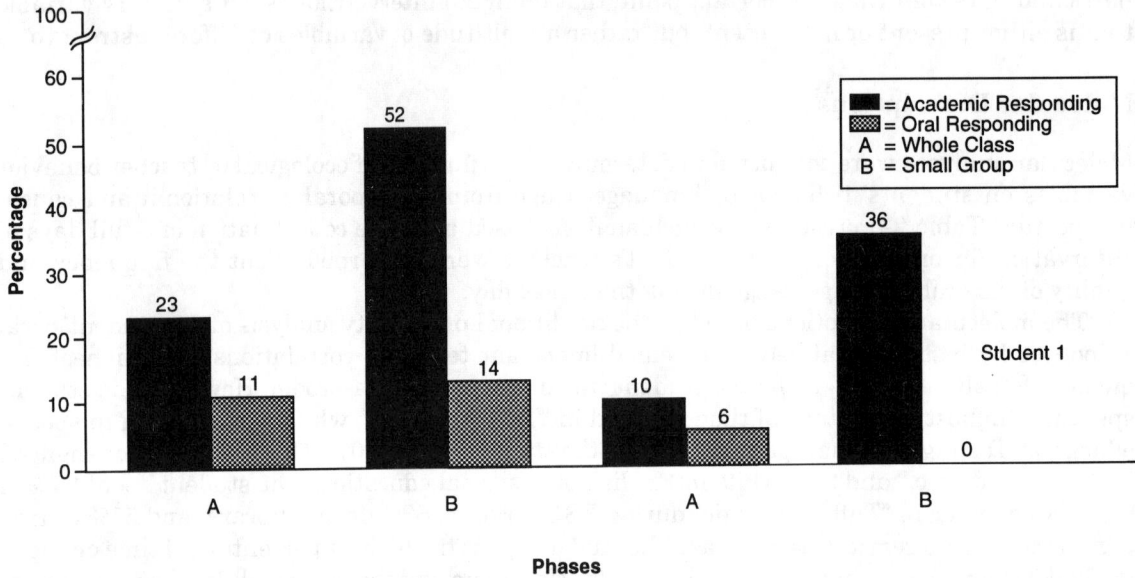

instruction provided a significant ecological change resulting in a higher active engagement level of the student's activity-related behaviors but in itself was not a causal factor for increased language usage (see Table 2-6).

TABLE 2-6

ESCRIBE: Output Validation of Intervention Changes

Student Variable	Whole Class	Small Group
Activity-Related Responses		
Writing	3	18
Reading Aloud	1	0
Reading Silent	0	14
Talk	6	9
Other Academic	5	6
Nonacademic	1	8
Noncompliance	1	11
Attention	83	34
None	0	0
Academic Responding	15	47
Oral Responding	7	10

In summation, these analyses presented the use of an ecobehavioral assessment approach to determine the impact of ecological and teacher variables on student behaviors. Molecular analyses such as this provide critical direction in the development of interventions and in evaluating effects across a broad array of variables. These scores, paired with student outcome measures, can provide a detailed picture of classroom processes that are most highly related to academic and linguistic programmatic success.

SUMMARY

We have described a powerful methodological improvement for use in the next generation of bilingual and bilingual special education efficacy studies—an approach for generating the data necessary to support instructional or accountability research in bilingual special education programs. The ecobehavioral approach will expand the focus of assessment to account for both the independent and dependent variables to explain student outcomes. This type of evaluation would enable us to design, deliver, and support the most effective educational programs for this unique and diverse population, a far superior system than the typical single-case analysis currently used.

REFERENCES

Ambert, A., & Dew, N. (1983). *Special education for exceptional bilingual students: A handbook for educators.* Dallas, TX: Evaluation, Dissemination and Assessment Center.

Arreaga-Mayer, C., & Greenwood, C. R. (1986). Environmental variables affecting the school achievement of culturally and linguistically different learners: An instructional perspective. *Journal of the National Association for Bilingual Education* (NABE), *10*(2), 113–136.

Baca, L., & Bransford, J. (1982). *An appropriate education for handicapped children with limited English proficiency.* An ERIC exceptional child education report. Reston, VA: ERIC Clearinghouse on Handicapped and Gifted Children.

Baca, L., & Cervantes, H. (1984). *The bilingual special education interface.* St. Louis: Times Mirror/Mosby.

Baer, D. M., Wolf, M. M., & Risley, T. R. (1987). Some still current dimensions of applied behavior analysis. *Journal of Applied Behavior Analysis, 20*, 313–327.

Baker, K., & DeKanter, A. (1981). *Effectiveness of bilingual education: A review of the literature.* Washington, DC: Final report to the White House Regulatory Analysis and Review Group, Office of Planning, Budget and Evaluation.

Barker, R. G., & Wright, P. E. (1968). *Ecological psychology: Concepts and methods for studying the environment of human behavior.* Stanford, CA: Stanford University Press.

Bernal, E. M. (1983). Trends in bilingual special education. *Learning Disability Quarterly, 6*, 424–431.

Bijou, S. W., Patterson, R. F., & Ault, M. H. (1968). A method to integrate descriptive and experimental field studies at the level of data and empirical concept. *Journal of Applied Behavior Analysis, 1*, 175–191.

Bronfenbrenner, U. (1979). Contexts of child rearing: Problems and prospects. *American Psychologist, 34*, 844–850.

Brophy, J., & Good, T. L. (1986). Teacher behavior and student achievement. In M. L. Wittrock (Ed.), *Handbook of research on teaching* (3rd ed.), (pp. 328–375). New York: Macmillan.

Carta, J. J., & Greenwood, C. R. (1985). Ecobehavioral assessment: A methodology for expanding the evaluation of early intervention programs. *Topics in Early Childhood Education, 5*, 88–104.

Carta, J. J., Greenwood, C. R., & Robinson, S. L. (1987). Application of an ecobehavioral approach to the evaluation of early intervention programs. In R. Prinz (Ed.), *Advances in behavioral assessment of children and families* (Vol. 3, pp. 123–155). Greenwich, CT: JAI.

Cortes, L. A. (1977, April). *Students' reaction to bilingual special education.* Paper presented at the Annual International Convention of The Council for Exceptional Children, Atlanta. (ED 139 174)

Cummins, J. (1983). Bilingualism and special education: Programs and pedagogical issues. *Learning Disability Quarterly, 6,* 373–386.

Danoff, M., Coles, G., McLaughlin, D., & Reynolds, D. (1977a). *Evaluation of the impact of SEA Title VII Spanish-English bilingual education programs: Vol. 1. Study designs and interim findings.* Palo Alto, CA: American Institutes of Research. (ED 138–090)

Danoff, M., Coles, G., McLaughlin, D., & Reynolds, D. (1977b). *Evaluation of the impact of SEA Title VII Spanish-English bilingual education programs: Vol. II. Project descriptions.* Palo Alto, CA: American Institutes of Research. (ED 138 091)

Danoff, M., Coles, G., McLaughlin, D., & Reynolds, D. (1978a). *Evaluation of the impact of SEA Title VII Spanish-English bilingual education programs: Vol III. Year two impact data, educational process, and in depth analyses.* Palo Alto, CA: American Institutes of Research. (ED 154 635)

Danoff, M., Coles, G., McLaughlin, D., & Reynolds, D. (1978b). *Evaluation of the impact of SEA Title VII Spanish-English bilingual education programs: Overview of study and findings.* Palo Alto, CA: American Institutes of Research. (ED 154 634)

De La Garza, J., & Medina, M. (1985). Academic achievements as influenced by bilingual instruction for Spanish-dominant Mexican American children. *Hispanic Journal of Behavioral Sciences, 7*(3), 247–259.

Dunkin, M. J., & Biddle, B. J. (1974). *The study of teaching.* New York: Holt, Rinehart & Winston.

Fradd, S., & Hallman, C. L. (1983). Implications of psychological and educational research for assessment and instruction of culturally and linguistically different students. *Learning Disability Quarterly, 6,* 468–478.

Greenwood, C. R., Carta, J. J., & Atwater, J. (1991). Ecobehavioral analysis in the classroom. *Journal of Behavioral Education, 1,* 59–77.

Greenwood, C. R., Carta, J. J., Kamps, D., & Arreaga-Mayer, C. (1990). Ecobehavioral analysis of classroom instruction. In S. R. Schroeder (Ed.), *Ecobehavioral analysis and developmental disabilities* (pp. 33–63). New York: Springer-Verlag.

Greenwood, C. R., Delquadri, J., & Hall, R. V. (1984). Opportunity to respond and student academic performance. In W. L. Heward, L. E. Heron, J. Trap-Porter, & D. S. Hill (Eds.), *Focus on behavior analysis in education.* Columbus, OH: Merrill.

Greenwood, C. R., Delquadri, J., Stanley, S., Sasso, G., Whorton, D., & Schulte, D. (1981, Summer). Allocating opportunity to learn as a basis for academic remediation. *Monograph for Children with Severe Behavior Disorders,* 22–23.

Hakuta, K. (1985). *Mirrors of language: A debate on bilingualism.* New York: Basic.

Maheady, L. (1985). The assessment of the bilingual exceptional child: Trends and models. In L. Baca, J. Starks, & E. Hartley (Eds.), *Third annual symposium: Exceptional Hispanic children and youth. Monograph Series, 6*(1), 41–63. Boulder, CO: Bueno Center for Multicultural Education.

Maheady, L., Towne, R., Algozzine, B., Mercer, J., & Ysseldyke, J. (1983). Minority overrepresentation: A case for alternative practices prior to referral. *Learning Disability Quarterly, 6,* 448–457.

Medina, M., Saldate, M., & Mishra, S. (1985). The sustaining effects of bilingual instruction: A follow-up study. *Journal of Instructional Psychology, 12*(3), 132–139.

Ochoa, A. M., Pacheco, R., & Omark, D. R. (1983). Addressing the learning disability needs of limited English proficient students: Beyond language and race. *Learning Disability Quarterly, 6,* 416–423.

O'Malley, J. M. (1978). Review of the evaluation of the impact of SEA Title VII Spanish/English bilingual education program. *Bilingual Research, 1,* 6–10.

Ortiz, A., & Yates, J. R. (1983). Incidents of exceptionality among Hispanics: Implications for manpower planning. *Journal of the National Association for Bilingual Education* (NABE), *7*(3), 41–54.

Public Law No. 94-142. (1975). *Federal Register.* Washington, DC: U. S. Government Printing Office.

Rogers-Warren, A. K., & Warren, S. F. (1977). *Ecological perspective in behavior analysis.* Baltimore: University Park Press.

Saldate, M. IV, Mishra, S., & Medina, M. (1985). Bilingual instruction and academic achievement: A longitudinal study. *Journal of Instructional Psychology, 12*(1), 24–30.

Stanley, S. O., & Greenwood, C. R. (1983). *Code for instructional structure and student academic response (CISSAR): Observer's manual.* Kansas City: Juniper Gardens Children's Project, University of Kansas.

Thurlow, M. L., Ysseldyke, J. E., Graden, J., & Algozzine, B. (1984). Opportunity to learn for LD students receiving different levels of special education services. *Learning Disabilities Quarterly, 7,* 55–67.

Tikunoff, W. (1983). *An emerging description of successful bilingual instruction: Executive summary of Part I of the SBIF study* (NIE Contract No. 400-80-0026). San Francisco: Far West Laboratory for Educational Research and Development.

Trueba, H., Guthrie, G., & Au, K. (1981). *Culture and the bilingual classroom.* Rowley, MA: Newbury House.

Tymitz, B. L. (1983). Bilingual special education: A challenge to evaluation practices. In D. R. Omark & J. G. Erickson (Eds.), *The bilingual exceptional child* (pp. 359–377). San Diego: College-Hill.

Willig, A. C. (1981). The effectiveness of bilingual education: Review of a report. *Journal of the National Association for Bilingual Education* (NABE), *6*(2–3), 1–20.

Willig, A. (1985). A meta-analysis of selected studies on the effectiveness of bilingual education. *Review of Educational Research, 55*(3), 269–317.

Wolf, R. L. (1978). *Policy implications of bilingual special education.* Bloomington: Indiana Center for Evaluation, Indiana University.

Ysseldyke, J. E., Thurlow, M. L., Mecklenburg, C., Graden, J., & Algozzine, B. (1984). Changes in academic engaged time as a function of assessment and special education intervention. *Special services in the schools* (Vol. 1, 2). New York: Haworth.

CHAPTER 3

Assessment of Asian and Pacific Islander Students for Gifted Programs

Li-Rong Lilly Cheng
Kenji Ima
Gene Labovitz

The population of the United States is becoming more linguistically, ethnically, socially, and religiously diverse. By the turn of the century, one third of all citizens will be members of ethnic and multicultural groups, as will one third of the nation's public school students (American Council on Education, 1988). At present, in 25 of our largest metropolitan areas half or more than half of the public school students come from diverse ethnic and multicultural groups. By the year 2000, 42% of public school students in the metropolitan areas will be from these groups. This change in the composition of our population will have significant effects on schools and their ability to produce an educated workforce. This chapter concentrates on the assessment of Asian and Pacific Islander students for gifted programs.

Asians have been immigrating to the United States for at least 200 years. However, before 1965 relatively few Asians migrated to this country because immigration laws restricted their admission. In 1965, United States immigration laws changed, resulting in a dramatic increase in the number of Asian immigrants. In addition, conflict in Southeast Asia generated over a million refugees who gained admission to this country. The most prominent groups represented are from Cambodia (Kampuchea), China (Taiwan, Hong Kong, and the People's Republic of China), India, Japan, Korea, Laos, the Philippines, and Vietnam. There has been a steady but lesser influx of Pacific Islanders, especially Guamanians and Samoans. Hawaiians who come to the U.S. mainland are internal migrants (Cheng, 1991).

Asians and Pacific Islanders collectively are the fastest growing ethnic and multicultural community in this country. The 1990 Census data reported over 7 million Asians and Pacific Islanders living in the United States. The current number represents 2.9% of the population, as compared to 1.5% or 3 million people in 1980. Asians and Pacific Islanders are expected to constitute 4% of the population by the year 2000—a projected growth of 400% in 30 years (Gardner, Robey, & Smith, 1985). Excluding Hawaii, California shows the largest growth in Asian and Pacific Islander population. In 1990, Asians and Pacific Islanders constituted 9.6% of California's population—a 127% increase in 10 years (O'Hare & Felt, 1991). Not only the size, but the diversity of that population is noteworthy; many groups have little identification with each other as Asian Americans. The pooling of diverse peoples into a single category reflects the arbitrary use of geographic origins as a criterion for grouping people for various political and bureaucratic decisions such as determination of equal representation.

Even though some commonalities exist among Asians and Pacific Islanders, they are a diverse population. They speak different languages, practice different religions, and hold different views. The five main language families and some of their important languages are Malayo-Polynesian

(Chamorro, Illocano, Tagalog), Sino-Tibetan (Thai, Yao, Mandarin, Cantonese), Austro-Asiatic (Khmer, Vietnamese, Hmong), Papuan (New Guinean), and Altaic (Japanese, Korean) (Ma, 1985). Asians and Pacific Islanders who emigrate to the U.S. have various bilingual and biliterate backgrounds. Another important variable is the religious/philosophical beliefs of the individual or family. The major religious/philosophical systems are Buddhism, Confucianism, Taoism, Shintoism, Animism, Catholicism, and Islam (Cheng, 1989).

Despite the differences, it is imperative that educators begin to understand the many cultures that their students bring into the classroom because these cultures will affect learning and placement decisions, such as the decisions on gifted classification. While there are numerous studies available on gifted students and programs, few exist for ethnic and multicultural groups (Maker & Schiever, 1989), and even fewer have focused on Asian students. Very few studies focus on the Southeast Asian students who are refugees or those born in the United States of refugee parents. In an attempt to reduce stereotyping and overgeneralization, a brief description of the major Asian and Pacific Islander groups follows.

MAJOR CULTURAL AND ETHNIC GROUPS

Chinese

Chinese people first immigrated to the United States over 100 years ago and constitute the largest Asian group, with over 1.6 million persons. Although the majority of the early migrants came from the rural areas of Canton, recently Chinese persons have come from Hong Kong, mainland China, and Taiwan to study, to join families, or for economic purposes. Although the Chinese from other countries such as Vietnam and Laos are counted as Vietnamese nationals, they constitute significant portions of immigrants and refugees classified as Southeast Asians—persons from non-Chinese soil.

The Chinese culture places heavy emphasis on the family as a unit, and each family member has a well-defined role. If a family member is successful, the entire family receives credit, although accomplishments are downplayed because expressions of pride are considered arrogance. Since parents expect excellence, they do not often praise children. Outward calm, control of one's emotions, harmony, filial piety, and humility are virtues valued by the Chinese. In traditional Chinese families, teachers are highly respected. If a child does poorly in school, the parents see it as a reflection of their own failure. The Chinese people speak more than 80 different languages, not counting the hundreds of dialects and variations of those languages. Some are closely related, while others are mutually unintelligible (Tseng, 1990). The two main dialects spoken by the Chinese in the United States are Cantonese and Mandarin (the national language).

Koreans

Korea borders China and Russia and is adjacent to Japan. Korea was a Chinese colony until 668 A.D., when the Silla Kingdom was formed, unifying all Korean people. In 1910 Korea became a Japanese colony. At the end of World War II, when Japan was defeated, North and South Korea were formed (Cheng, 1991). In 1950, North Korea invaded South Korea, beginning the Korean War, which ended with a Communist regime in the North (Kim, 1978).

Although Korean immigration began in the early 1900s, the majority of Korean Americans are of relatively recent origin. Since 1975, Koreans have been migrating to the United States from South Korea in large numbers. The Korean educational system is patterned after the U.S. system, although the traditional underpinnings remain Confucian. Children are raised in an environment in which going to the best schools is highly valued. They are accustomed to working hard to obtain high scores on college entrance examinations, reflecting the long-standing Chinese influence on Korean attitudes toward schooling. The Chinese culture has influenced the behavior of the Koreans, who espouse its emphasis on harmony, reverence for elders, social order, and fairness

(Chu, 1990). Recent immigrants are even more highly educated than earlier immigrants, since the increase in the Korean standard of living and progress in education have been substantial in recent decades.

Japanese

Japan comprises four main islands and more than 500 islets. It is the most densely populated country in the world, with a population of over 115 million, the majority living along the coast. Japanese people began to emigrate to the United States in large numbers between 1891 and 1907. In 1924, further immigration was stopped. The majority of Japanese Americans are descended from that early cohort, even though migration restarted after World War II. Although some children of Japanese descent in the United States are native Japanese speakers, the majority are U.S.-born and primary speakers of English. In 1960 they were the largest single U.S.-based Asian group, but now they are the fifth largest Asian group, being eclipsed by rapid growth in the numbers of Chinese, Filipinos, Koreans, and Vietnamese.

Japanese families value obedience, dependence on family, and restraint in the expression of emotions. As in other Asian families, the family members have well-defined roles. Japanese children are expected to be obedient, respectful, and well behaved. Elderly people are revered. The emphasis on education remains in force among those who are American born.

Filipinos

The Philippines is an archipelago of more than 7,200 islands situated south of China and southeast of Indochina. The distance between islands and a long history of provincialism make it difficult for Filipinos to think of themselves as a unitary people (Cheng & Ima, 1990). Spain gained control of the islands in 1521, naming them after King Philip of Spain. The islands were ceded to the United States at the end of the Spanish-American War. During World War II, Japan took over the Philippines. The United States granted the Philippines its independence after the Japanese were defeated in World War II. Although the first Filipinos arrived on the North American continent before American independence, larger numbers arrived early in this century and the vast majority arrived after 1965, reflecting the changed U.S. immigration policy. With the continued connection to the United States through such resources as the recruitment of Philippines nationals into the U.S. Navy, Filipinos are likely to become numerically the largest Asian/Pacific Islander immigrant group by the turn of the century. The 1965 immigration law favored admission of more highly educated persons, resulting in a high proportion of professionally trained workers.

The repeated colonization of the Philippines has made their culture a mixture of East and West. The family is seen as a family *unit,* but it is not based on the patrilineal model of the Chinese. Rather, the Filipinos have a bilateral family system in which the individuals are obligated to both maternal and paternal sides of the family (Galang, Noble, & Halog, 1985). Although the extended family is common, family patterns, practices, and values differ according to the area in which the families live, religious affiliation, ethnic group membership, and socioeconomic status (Cheng, 1991).

The Filipino people believe in education as a path to success, and they respect scholars. Thus, parents encourage their children to do well in school and to perfect their English skills (Monzon, 1984). The exact number of Philippines languages is uncertain, but there are three major languages: Tagalog, spoken by 25% of the population; Illocano, spoken by 16%; and Visayan, spoken by 44%. The Philippines census of 1970 listed 75 mother tongues. Since the study of English has been part of the Filipino educational system since the turn of the last century, the vast majority of immigrant Filipino students can speak English. Thus, unlike other Asian groups, they have arrived for the most part speaking English and preacculturated to American customs. Nevertheless, it is easy to underestimate the gaps between Filipino and American language and culture.

Southeast Asians: Vietnamese, Khmer, Lao, and Hmong

There were relatively few Southeast Asians in the United States before 1975. Since that time, over a million Southeast Asian refugees have arrived in this country. Southeast Asia is positioned geographically between two major Asian civilizations—China and India—and this has important cultural and historical implications. Most Americans assume that Southeast Asia is simply an extension of the Chinese cultural sphere of influence, failing to recognize the impact of Indian civilization in this region. The division of the two major civilizations is between Vietnam (influenced predominantly by China) and Cambodia/Laos (influenced predominantly by India). The resulting approach to schooling differs, with individuals from the Chinese-influenced areas being more preoccupied with degrees and the other formal markings of education. The refugee background of Southeast Asians differentiates them from Asian immigrants on at least two counts. First, they are fleeing political persecution rather than pursuing economic gains. Associated with their flight is war trauma, which is often manifested in emotional troubles such as depression and nightmares. Second, although there is some selectivity of more energetic individuals among Southeast Asian refugees, these groups are more likely to contain individuals with less educational and occupational experience than Asian immigrants as a whole, reflecting less selectivity and less preparedness to adjust to a modern and fast-changing society. Indeed, many have little schooling and bring with them occupational skills that are inappropriate for modern economies (e.g., preindustrial farmers).

Vietnamese. The Chinese ruled Vietnam for a thousand years until Vietnam gained its independence. In the latter half of the 19th century, the French conquered Vietnam, and they ruled until 1954, when Vietnam was divided into North and South Vietnam under the Geneva Agreement. In spite of the Agreement, conflict continued until 1975, when the Communists took control of the country. The result was an unprecedented flight of Vietnamese from their country. Three different waves of Vietnamese refugees have come to the United States. The first were those who left in 1975; these were principally persons from the educated ranks. The second wave included individuals representing a wider range of Vietnamese people, including those with less education; they were labeled "boat people" because their flight frequently involved departing by boat. The third and more recent wave includes both the continuing flight from political and economic problems and "orderly departure" migrants who have been granted legal permission to leave Vietnam. They form the largest Southeast Asian group, numbering over 600,000 persons.

The Vietnamese place a strong emphasis on the family, with members living and working together under a paternal structure. Older children have the responsibility for their younger siblings, and, in general, children are taught to respect their parents and elders—reflecting the Confucian tradition. There is a great emphasis on family hierarchy and social order. Education is of extreme importance to the Vietnamese people and holds an honored place in their society. Most children in Vietnam attend public schools. Among Southeast Asians refugees, the Vietnamese are the most educated group. Consequently, as a group, they are the most likely to succeed academically. The education system is teacher-oriented and based upon memorization and repetition.

Khmer. Cambodia, also known as Kampuchea, is located in mainland Southeast Asia. It was at its historical zenith from the 11th to the 13th centuries, when the monumental Ankgor Wat was constructed. France colonized the region in the late 19th century although not with the intensity of cultural imposition that occurred in Vietnam. Thus Cambodia retained more of its traditional ways until recently.

In 1953 Cambodia gained independence, but 16 years later, in the midst of the Vietnam War, it became embroiled in the conflict that spawned the Khmer Rouge and the infamous Pol Pot era—a period often compared with the Jewish Holocaust because between 1.5 and 2 million Cambodians out of a population of 8 million were either murdered, starved, or died as a result of poor medical care. In 1979 the Vietnamese Communists defeated the Khmer Rouge, resulting in a large refugee outflow. Although the majority remain in Southeast Asia, the United States has received over 200,000 Cambodians. Many families arrived in this country as refugees with a history of trauma that defies the imagination. It is estimated that half of the adults remain in psychological crisis. Among all refugee groups, they have the most severe disruption of family life—an estimated 25% of adult females are widows. This refugee experience must be addressed above and beyond even cultural considerations. Even though the Cambodians shared many of the same experiences as other refugees, their level of suffering exceeded that of the others. The educational consequences of these experiences include higher school dropout rates (Rumbaut & Ima, 1988). This emphasizes that educators need to pay heed to the particulars of students rather than assume that they belong to some monolithic Asian group.

The cultural base of Cambodian society is Indian, as reflected in the Sanskrit-based writing system and the religious ideas of Theravada Buddhism. Therefore it is a mistake to assume a kinship to Chinese, Japanese, or Korean cultures.

Lao. Laos is situated south of China, north of Cambodia, east of Thailand and Burma, and west of Vietnam. Laos is divided between the dominant Lao and minorities, including the Hmong. The French ruled Laos from the end of the 19th century until independence was granted in 1949. In 1975, along with the non-Communist governments of Cambodia and Vietnam, Laos fell to the Communists, resulting in the departure of many Laotians toward the Thai border. As a consequence, the Laotian population decreased significantly, from 3.5 million to 2 million. From the border refugee camps, approximately 150,000 Lao were resettled in the United States.

Generally the Lao have large families with extended family households. They, like the Cambodians, have deep cultural roots in the traditions of India—including their writing system, religion, and schooling. Their level of education is approximately the same as that of the Cambodians—roughly 5 to 6 years of formal schooling on the average. Many received their education in the village pagoda, which emphasized religion rather than Western notions of education. In the decades prior to the departure of the refugees, the government had embarked on a massive education campaign, but it had yet to raise the average level of literacy to one approximating that of Western societies.

Hmong. Although the Hmong were originally from China, they moved to the mountainous area of Indochina as late as the 19th century. During the Vietnam conflict, many Hmong joined forces with the United States in fighting Communist forces. With the defeat of the non-Communist forces, they were marked for retribution, forcing many to leave Laos. Before their evacuation in 1975, most Hmong had never been away from their mountain homes. There are approximately 90,000 Hmong now living in the United States (Cheng, 1991).

The Hmong view of education is quite different from that of other refugee groups, for they relied primary on an oral and nonliterate tradition. Among all refugees, and indeed among all Asian immigrants/refugees, they are probably the least formally educated group. In spite of that background, they do understand the benefits of a good education. They realize that education leads to job opportunities and employment, but, given the recency of their engagement with formal schooling, they have a wide gap to bridge.

Pacific Islanders

The Pacific Islands are grouped into three clusters: Polynesia, Melanesia, and Micronesia. Most numerous among the Islanders are the Hawaiians, Samoans, and Chamorros, in that order. Islander families place great emphasis on authority. Families may be patrilineal or matrilineal. They are usually extended and may include three generations living together.

Their primary and secondary education systems are similar to those in the United States. However, different emphasis is placed on characteristics such as being on time, having good attendance records, and completing projects. Teachers are well respected, and children attempt to please their teachers. Among the 5 million inhabitants of the Pacific Islands, over 1,200 indigenous languages are spoken. The five *lingua francas* used by the Pacific Islanders are

French, English, Pidgin, Spanish, and Bahasa Indonesian. Multicultural sources heavily influence the languages. Also, different cultures place emphasis on certain groups of words. For example, in the Chamorro, Carolinian, and Marshalese languages there are many words for the differing stages of the coconut (Cheng & Ima, 1989).

These descriptions allude to the diversity among Asians and Pacific Islander people—variations in language, customs, family arrangements, histories, exposure to the West, and immigration to the United States. Their school performances also vary, reflecting differences in factors such as the premigration level of schooling of their parents.

REFERRAL TO GIFTED PROGRAMS

Eggleston (1977) defined education's hidden curriculum as the tacit values, attitudes, and unofficial rules of behavior students must learn to participate and succeed in school. Those values, attitudes, and unofficial rules operate in every classroom, and they are learned and absorbed by both teachers and students. A conflict exists when teachers and students do not share the same rules and values. Teachers may not be aware of the values, since they have internalized them through their own socialization process. Cheng (1991) pointed out that certain Asian and Pacific Islander values are diametrically opposed to Western values—for example, being vocal and competitive rather than quiet and collaborative. Such hidden agendas may lead a teacher to recommend that students be tested for giftedness or, conversely, discourage a teacher from recommending such testing.

Maker and Schiever (1989) have suggested that cultural differences affect immigrant children, but what evidence do we have on cultural differences that affect the identification of Asian and Pacific Islander students as gifted? Do cultural stereotypes interfere with the assessment of giftedness even in the face of test evidence? And what of the problems surrounding bilingualism, including a low level of proficiency in the English language? Does limited proficiency in English prevent identification of giftedness? What implications might be suggested by evidence surrounding the answers to these questions?

Academic Performance of Asian and Pacific Islanders in San Diego: A Case Study

Test performance is correlated with several factors such as ethnicity, country of origin, length of stay in the United States, and social class. Ima and Rumbaut (1989) found diverse results in studying the relationship between school performance and language background of non-English-speaking and bilingual students. Asian and Pacific Islanders ranged from high to low levels of schooling achievement. However, in general, they performed above average when measured by their grade point averages.

The following data are taken from a recent study by Ima and Labovitz (1991) on the test performance of secondary students of the San Diego Unified School District. The district is the second largest school district in the state of California and eighth in the nation. The data on approximately 24,000 secondary school students in grades 7 through 12 were gathered from school files, making it possible to develop statistical benchmarks for the assessment of minority students.

We examined the results of the Comprehensive Tests of Basic Skills (CTBS), a widely used standardized measure to gauge students' educational achievement. The tests are intended for national use, to measure systematically those skills that are prerequisite to studying and learning in school, classified under five broad skill areas: recognition, translation, interpretation, application, and analysis. The CTBS produces raw scores in seven different areas or subtests: Reading Vocabulary, Reading Comprehension, Language Expression, Spelling, Language Mechanics, Mathematics Computation, and Mathematics Concepts and Applications. The raw scores are converted into percentile numbers. These subtest scores, in turn, are averaged to produce three composite indices of achievement, measuring *Reading* (combining the Vocabulary and Comprehension subtests), *Language* (combining Language Expression and Language Mechanics), and *Mathematics* (combining Computation and Mathematics Concepts and Applications). The results of these achievement tests provide data that may be compared nationally with other student groups at similar grade levels. In this report we cite student scores in the three composite indices of reading, language, and mathematics.

Figure 3-1 presents the mean percentile scores of each ethnic group separately for reading, language, and mathematics. The ethnic rank orders vary with each CTBS component. The rank orders, for the most part, fit the common-sense image of student performances, particularly the high averages of Asian students. This ranking also fits Ogbu and Matute-Bianchi's thesis (1986) regarding the differences between caste-like (Native American, Pacific Islanders, Hispanic, and African-American) and immigrant (Asian, Filipino, and Southeast Asian) students (Ima & Labovitz, 1991). Ogbu and Matute-Bianchi (1986) differentiated between the "caste-like status" or subordination of the African American and the "immigrant status" of newer students of color such as the Asians. The separation of the Asian groups from Pacific Islanders presents an initial glimpse into the diversity of Asian and Pacific Islanders. These variations in CTBS scores correspond to variations in the likelihood of being classified as gifted, which we will examine later.

Asian students perform above average on mathematics test scores, but they consistently have much lower verbal scores. Southeast Asians have the most highly mixed test performances. They are both similar and dissimilar to other Asian students, reflecting the differences in background experiences—especially the differences based on refugee versus immigrant status. On the one hand they have above average mathematics scores, but on the other hand the lowest reading scores. Pacific Islanders, have consistently low scores in all three areas.

The entire student population forms two clusters on math scores—those with higher scores include Asians, Filipinos, Southeast Asians, and whites, and those with lower scores include Pacific Islanders, Latinos, and African Americans. These results indicate not only that many Asian students are able to perform well in spite of their unfamiliarity with the English language, but perhaps more importantly, that significant variations exist among Asians and Pacific Islanders overall and on individual test areas.

FIGURE 3-1

CTBS Scores by Ethnicity

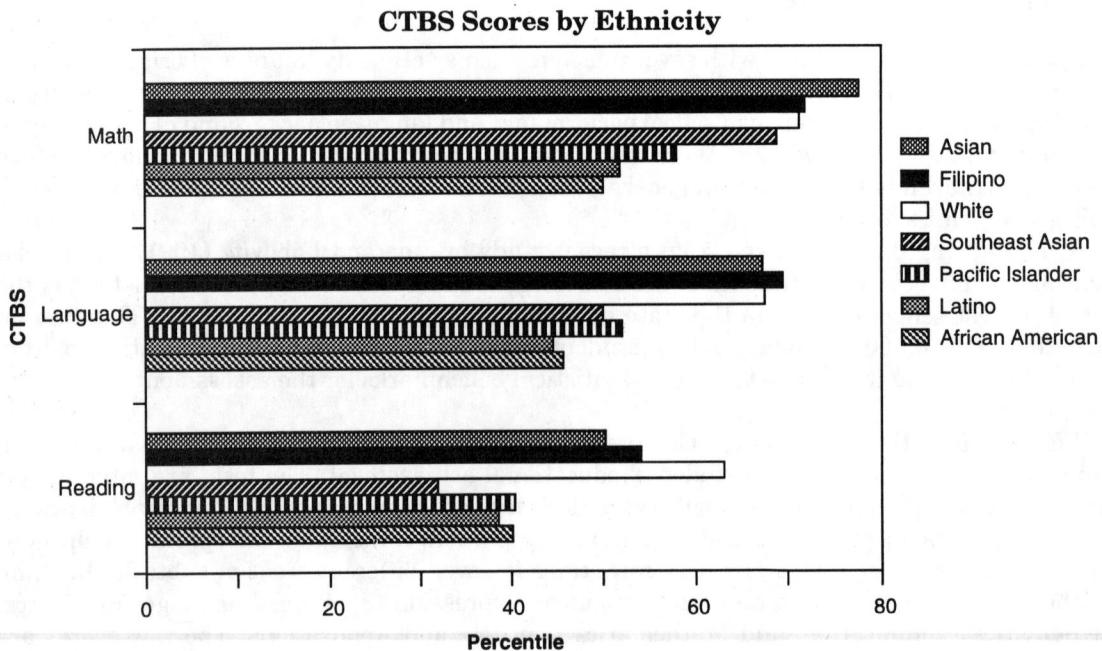

36

The reading scores, in contrast to the mathematics scores, reveal a generally lower overall level for all Asian groups, but the mathematics-reading gap is greatest among Southeast Asians. Whites had high reading scores, Asians and Filipinos had moderate scores, and Pacific Islanders, African Americans, Latinos, and Southeast Asians had the lowest scores (see Table 3-1). Although all three CTBS scores are highly related to grade point average among all students, mathematics is more highly related to class grades than reading. This suggests the greater importance of mathematics scores than reading scores in predicting grades.

Southeast Asians, the most recently arrived group, have the lowest reading scores among all groups, suggesting the importance of the length of residence in the United States for students regardless of ethnicity. For newcomers, reading is the most important subject; however, mathematics is a more accurate measure of a newcomer's academic potential, and therefore most relevant for gifted identification. For groups who traditionally do well, such as Asians, the mathematics score is an excellent identifier of giftedness, and should be used even with students who have low reading scores (Ima & Labovitz, 1991).

The program for gifted students in the San Diego Unified School District is the Gifted and Talented Education (GATE) program. Two major measures were recently employed to meet the commitment to achieve equity for students with culturally and linguistically diverse backgrounds. First, testers used identification instruments that are more likely to identify giftedness in diverse populations. Second, teachers were trained to identify and develop potentially gifted students. They were encouraged to create classroom environments and develop strategies that encourage high-level thinking. These measures increased the number of previously underrepresented nonwhite students, but curiously they ignored in large part the issue of identifying students from backgrounds in which English was not the primary language.

TABLE 3-1

Mean CTBS Percentile Scores by Content Area, Racial/Ethnic Group, and Gender, Grades 7–12, San Diego Unified School District, 1989–1990

Content Area/ Gender	African American	Latino	Pacific Islander	Anglo	Filipino	Southeast Asian	Asian American	Total
Reading								
Male	38.0	37.2	38.5	62.4	53.5	32.0	55.8	49.0
Female	41.7	37.7	42.0	64.5	54.3	34.5	57.8	50.8
Total	39.9	37.5	40.2	63.4	53.9	33.2	56.8	49.9
N	4,719	5,552	199	10,420	2,864	2,483	683	27,059
Language								
Male	41.8	42.8	46.4	63.3	64.0	44.7	62.3	61.1
Female	51.2	49.3	59.3	70.6	71.8	53.1	69.6	53.7
Total	46.7	46.0	52.5	66.9	67.8	48.7	66.0	57.4
N	4,623	5,409	196	10,308	2,839	2,476	673	26,665
Mathematics								
Male	47.2	50.8	52.4	70.9	70.6	67.0	77.6	62.5
Female	49.5	50.3	61.7	71.3	73.2	66.5	77.5	62.9
Total	48.4	50.5	56.8	71.1	71.9	66.8	77.5	62.7
N	4,593	5,590	198	10,361	2,842	2,567	690	26,980

Source: San Diego Unified School District, Information Services Department.

Giftedness in Each Ethnic Group

Let us now examine the gifted among each ethnic group. Figure 3-2 displays the percentage of gifted students by ethnic group. These data are based on students who took the CTBS test and exclude those who for some reason did not take the test. In general, those who did not take the test were more likely to be at risk of school failure; consequently, their absence inflates the percentage of students who are classified as gifted. Nevertheless, the data provide a comparative portrait of the various ethnic groups and their likelihood of being identified as gifted. Figure 3-2 and Table 3-2 reveal that 28% of Asians, 20% of whites, 16% of Filipinos, 6% of Southeast Asians, 6% of African Americans, 6% of Pacific Islanders, and 5% of Latinos were placed in the gifted program. These results reveal a striking bimodal distribution, where the higher group is composed of Asian, white, and Filipino students and the lower group is composed of Southeast Asians, African Americans, Pacific Islanders, and Latinos. This pattern corresponds to the earlier observation of ethnic group differences on CTBS scores. All groups with high mathematics scores have a higher percentage of students identified as gifted, with the exception of Southeast Asians—their average mathematics scores are high, but their likelihood of being identified as gifted is low. Thus, ethnic variations reflect test performances, except among Southeast Asians. Is the fact of underrepresentation a reflection of the fact that many of them come from homes where English is not the primary language spoken?

Do we assess the potential of Asian and Pacific Islander gifted students unfairly? As suggested earlier, the majority of Asian and Pacific Islander students either were born outside the United States or have parents who are recent immigrants. Thus, fewer than half of all Asian and Pacific Islander students live in homes where English is the primary language. The identification of gifted students is based almost solely on paper-and-pencil instruments and teacher judgments, both biased toward English language competence. Hence, the higher association of gifted status with high reading and language test scores over mathematics scores is not surprising (Ima & Labovitz, 1991). Therefore we asked ourselves whether or not students from the various ethnic groups who performed at the highest two levels of the CTBS mathematics test (stanines 8 and 9) were equally likely to be identified as gifted. Indeed, for Latino and African-American students

FIGURE 3-2

Percent Gifted by Ethnicity

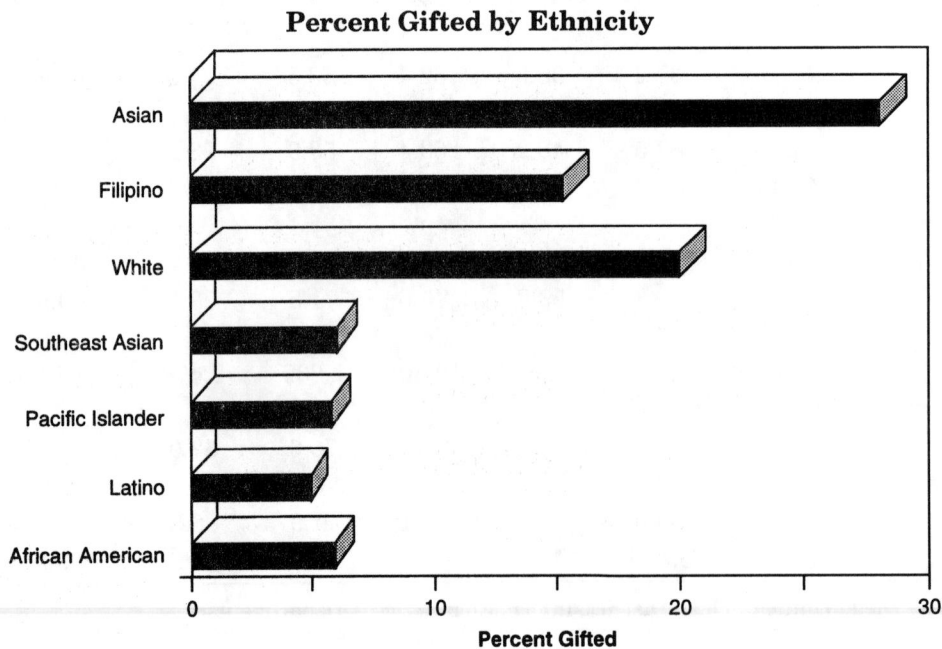

38

TABLE 3-2

Percent Gifted by Ethnicity and Language Status

| | Language Status | | | | |
Ethnicity	LEP	FEP	English Only	Total	N
Asian	9.6%	39.9%	30.1%	28.0%	1,170
Filipino	3.0	20.3	13.8	15.6	3,926
White	4.6	17.8	20.4	19.9	18,377
Southeast Asian	4.1	15.5	8.7	6.5	3,939
Pacific Islander	0.0	5.3	7.7	6.1	277
Latino	1.9	8.0	8.8	5.2	10,316
African American	1.1	5.6	6.4	6.3	6,953

LEP = limited English proficient; FEP = fluent English proficient.

who scored at the highest levels, their likelihood of being identified as gifted was similar to that of Filipino students, and although the gap between them and Asian and white students persisted, the relative difference was considerably diminished. Compare Figures 3-2 and 3-3. Only the Southeast Asian and Pacific Islander students who scored high in mathematics were markedly unlikely to be identified as gifted.

Since the numbers of Pacific Islanders are small, we are uncertain about the stability of their statistics, but the numbers of Southeast Asians are markedly higher (see Table 3-3). We suspect that the unusually low identification of Southeast Asians as gifted reflects both their relatively recent arrival and their limited English proficiency (LEP). Indeed, approximately two thirds of

FIGURE 3-3

Percent Gifted by Ethnicity Among High Math Performers

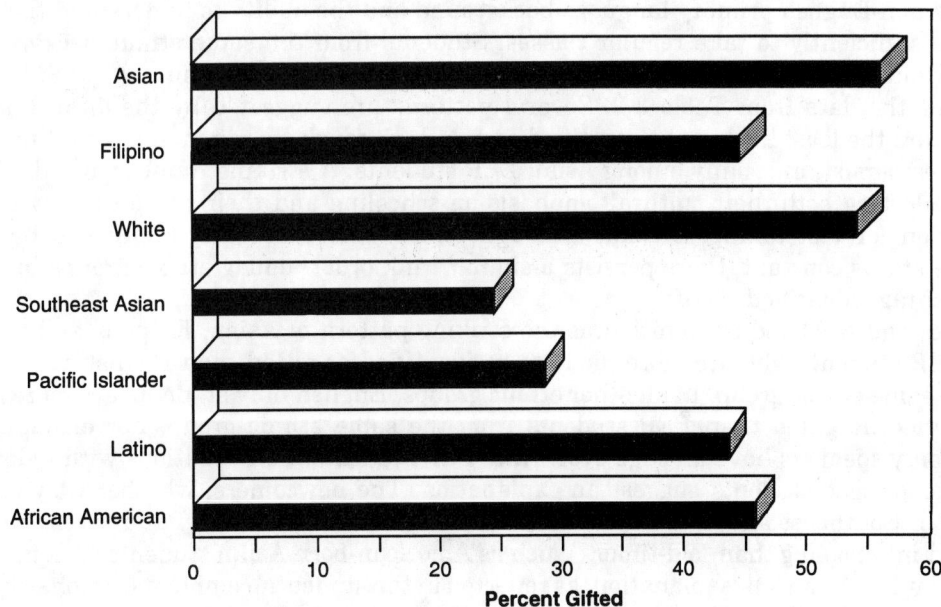

39

TABLE 3-3

Percent Gifted Among High Math Performers by Ethnicity

Ethnicity	Percent Gifted	N
Asian	56.4	303
Filipino	44.4	850
White	53.8	3,215
Southeast Asian	24.2	661
Pacific Islander	28.6	21
Latino	43.2	491
African American	45.8	297
Total high performers		5,347

Southeast Asian secondary students are classified as having limited English proficiency. Furthermore, it should be noted that the district does not have identification instruments for giftedness in any of the Southeast Asian languages, nor are teachers trained to deal with their languages in spite of special efforts to prepare teachers to identify more students of color for gifted programs.

Since the common measure of giftedness is also a measure of competence in the English language, one might ask how we can fairly test students from linguistically diverse backgrounds when they do not have English-language competence. The results indicate that these students often are not identified as gifted since identification of giftedness is largely based on reading scores, and their reading scores are low. There is a need to examine and challenge the notion of giftedness as correlated to reading scores, which undercuts chances that students from ethnic and cultural groups for whom English is not the primary language are classified as gifted. Indeed, our data indicate that higher GPAs are more likely to reflect high mathematics scores than high reading scores.

Table 3-2 indicates that LEP students are seriously underrepresented in the gifted category as compared to their counterparts who have fluent English proficiency (FEP)—individuals having the same non-English primary language background and the ability to understand the English language sufficiently to take regular classes. Students from the same ethnic background but whose primary language is English are identified as English only (EO) in Table 3-2. Figure 3-4 illustrates the data from Table 3-2. Several patterns are suggested by the data. First, LEP students are the least likely to be identified as gifted, although there remains a hint that ethnic differences persist, especially among Asian LEP students: A striking number are identified as gifted, reflecting both their cultural emphasis on schooling and their home country schooling preparation for test taking. Second, although ethnic differences are diminished by holding language status constant, there persists a similar rank order among ethnic groups in terms of the percentage identified as gifted.

Third, and a related observation, is the striking pattern of Asian, Filipino, and Southeast Asian FEP students who are more likely to be identified as gifted than English-only students from the same ethnic group. In all other ethnic groups, English-only students are more likely to be identified as gifted than FEP students from the same ethnic group. For example, white English-only speakers have an edge over white FEP students. Conversations with Asian immigrant and refugee students suggest an explanation. The newcomers, whether they be Asian, Filipino, or Southeast Asian, are more likely to take schooling seriously and invest more time and effort in schooling than "old-timers" such as American-born Asian students. It is interesting to note that the Asian folk explanation, as reflected in the students' comments, emphasizes effort rather than talent. This contrasts with the more common American folk explanation of "having

FIGURE 3-4

Percent Gifted by Ethnicity and Language Status

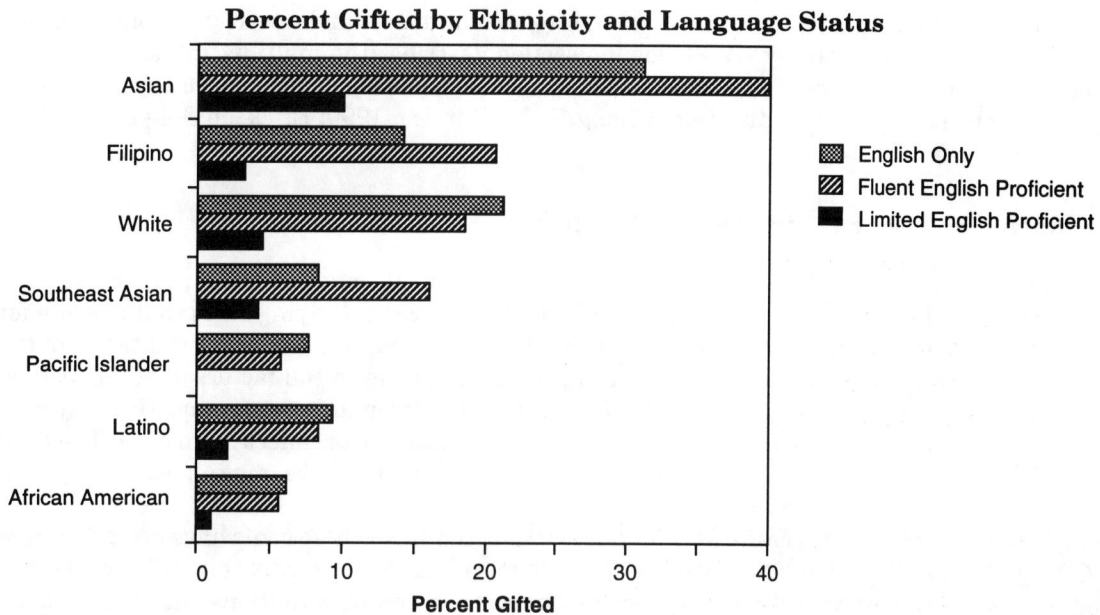

Legend:
- English Only
- Fluent English Proficient
- Limited English Proficient

X-axis: Percent Gifted (0, 10, 20, 30, 40)

Categories: Asian, Filipino, White, Southeast Asian, Pacific Islander, Latino, African American

smarts." Since the likelihood of being identified as gifted is greater for Asian immigrant students when compared to other ethnic groups, perhaps there is a cultural factor among Asian immigrants.

This observation, in conjunction with the statistical results, suggests that the identification of Asians as gifted is not a simple unitary phenomenon. In the first place, even given our limited data (note that we did not subdivide the Southeast Asians), we documented wide variations in the school performance and identification of gifted status of Asians and Pacific Islanders. Second, as suggested in our short Asian ethnic sketches, there are probably wide variations in attitudes, background preparation, and resources among Asians and Pacific Islanders that are associated with variations in schooling outcomes. Third, although there is consistency in identification of giftedness based on test scores, the identification favors verbal rather than mathematical indicators, precisely areas where Asians show greater weakness. In spite of the weakness in verbal areas, somehow many Asian students manage to outperform whites; what is even more striking is the superior performance of bilingual Asian students over monolingual English-speaking Asian students.

Perhaps these results vindicate our current schooling practices with these students, but we believe the results accrue in spite of teachers. We recognize the efforts and successes of newcomer Asian students, but the results suggest that educators may be overlooking areas for improvement in dealing with the identification of gifted Asian students. As suggested earlier in our reference to the hidden curriculum, Asian gifted students may be tapping part of that curriculum but we suspect it is one that is taken for granted by teachers. It is clearly an area that could be addressed more explicitly. Perhaps we have not given Asian students a fair break in the gifted identification process, especially among Southeast Asians and other recent newcomers.

IMPLICATIONS FOR PRACTITIONERS

A number of researchers have proposed a multidisciplinary approach to the assessment and identification of culturally and linguistically diverse populations (Kitano, 1991; Maker &

41

Schiever, 1989). Zappia (1989) proposed a case study approach that includes observations, interviews, formal tests, informal tests, and review of cumulative records. Her approach is based on the ethnographic methodology, which takes into account the ethnohistorical considerations of the individual child and family. The following section describes the multidisciplinary approach advocated by professionals from diverse disciplines of anthropology, psychology, sociology, linguistics, ethnography and education (Cheng, 1991; Damico, 1990; Erickson & Iglesias, 1986; Ortiz, 1990; Trueba, 1989).

Alternative Assessment Strategies Ethnography

In recent years educational assessment has been carried out through ethnographic techniques. Ethnography is the study of events and people in regard to the underlying rules that operate for the participants. The examiner must attempt to collect data that are truly representative of the student's repertoire; determine the cultural, linguistic, and experiential factors affecting behavior; and attempt to take the perspective of both the child and the mainstream educational system (Damico, 1990). Using naturalistic contexts enables the evaluator to collect more data. The data collected are also viewed through the perspective of the targeted culture, making the interpretation of the data less biased and more valid (Cheng, 1990).

Several ethnographic assessment procedures that accomplish these goals have been proposed by Cheng (1991). The student is observed over time in multiple contexts with a variety of interactants, thus determining his or her reactions to different situations and individuals. Successes, as well as difficulties, are recorded. The child's family members are interviewed to provide information regarding the child's background, home environment, current concerns, strengths and weaknesses, and home language usage. The evaluator also interacts with the student, being sensitive to the child's perspective and former experiences. Assessment procedures should be culturally and pragmatically appropriate for the child. The child's communication must be described in naturalistic environments with low anxiety and high motivation. Having the child describe experiences, retell stories, predict future events, and problem solve are all techniques that provide rich data for narrative analysis. Classroom teachers and aides can provide valuable information about the child's performance and behavior in various situations. Resource teachers can provide information about the child's performance in any special programs in which he or she is enrolled.

Dynamic Approach

Assessment must go beyond what the student has experienced to include the assessment of the child's current contextualization processes and ability to learn new contextualization rules. This is the dynamic approach (Gutierrez-Clellan, 1991). Feuerstein, Rand, Jensen, Kaniel, and Tzuriel (1987) proposed the assessment of learning potential or "modifiability" by preparing students for the challenges of assessment tasks. This approach focuses on exploration and probing and can help determine students' narrative development status and the means by which they could learn new narrative strategies. In essence, measures of modifiability are recommended. Dynamic assessments have indicated that the ability to transfer the newly learned skills to novel situations is the best predictor of an individual's competence (Campione & Brown, 1987). The effectiveness of dynamic assessment on the cognitive potentials of students from culturally and linguistically diverse groups has been supported by a number of researchers (Budoff, 1987; Feuerstein, 1980).

Portfolio

Nadeau (1991) has developed a portfolio assessment plan used in a public school system with a large population of LEP children. During the morning hours, ungraded homogeneous groupings of children with various language proficiency levels receive content instruction in their primary language. The afternoon programs are heterogeneous groupings, with students rotating among various content areas every 3 weeks. Examples of various types of childrens' work are collected at specific times during the year. Portfolios of the childrens' work, focusing on language arts, are maintained on a computer. Examples included may be book reports, stories, journals, creative writing, and accompanying art work. Each piece of work and the attached teacher comments are always available. Therefore, the portfolio may be used for ongoing assessment, assessment for giftedness, parent conferences, and school-wide assessment results.

Re-evaluating Mathematics Scores

Another alternative to ensure accuracy regarding assessment of the giftedness of students from non-English language backgrounds is the use of mathematics scores. Figure 3-3 revealed the underrepresentation of Southeast Asian and Pacific Islander students with high CTBS mathematics scores in the gifted program. Mathematics scores should be used for identification of gifted students. LEP students are clearly at a disadvantage when their high mathematics scores are not being considered. They are underrepresented because they have low English/literacy skills even though they may have extremely good mathematics scores.

Incidental Learning

Classroom teachers have the opportunity to observe students in different learning modes. *Incidental learning* refers to the learning that takes place without the teacher's deliberately trying to explain the content. Students who absorb information and can make inferences and problem solve are potential candidates for classification as gifted. Kayser (1991) indicated that it is possible that many college students from diverse ethnic and cultural groups are gifted even though they were not identified as gifted in primary school.

Teacher Observation and Recommendation

Teachers need to have high expectations of and promote the self-esteem of their students. Being a proactive teacher means promoting student learning by improving school climate (Valverde, 1988). Educators need to learn about the various cultures that their students bring into the classroom. The RISE Project (Rise to Individual Scholastic Excellence) (Borman & Spring, 1984) indicated that inappropriate school expectations, norms, practices, and policies account for the underachievement of a preponderance of students from low-income backgrounds and those from other ethnic and cultural groups. Andrews (1987) stated that when teachers have very positive perceptions of the workplace, their students show incremental growth in achievement. The teacher's self-perception as a change agent in empowering students is critical. Teachers' recommendations are key to students' identification as gifted. The referral of LEP students for gifted programs relies heavily on teacher recommendations.

A few years ago, there were hardly any Southeast Asian students in the GATE program. In recent years, there has been a slight increase of Southeast Asian LEP students in one San Diego school's GATE program through teacher referrals (A. Nadeau, personal communication, 1991).

CONCLUSION

We are experiencing marked demographic changes in student characteristics. This challenges educators to re-examine traditional educational solutions such as the identification of gifted students. We need to identify and encourage students of color to join the ranks of the gifted. The stereotype of Asians as high achievers is partially based on the reality of Asian student performances; however, reliance on the stereotype puts off the time when educators should be looking more closely at the teacher's role in the identification process. The brief examination of one school district's Asian and Pacific Islander students reveals a diversity of outcomes and suggests a complex set of factors that explain those outcomes.

But going beyond what students do, it is just as important to review the examiner's own world view, values, beliefs, way of life, communication style, learning style, cognitive style, and personal biases. Examiners must continually nurture their view of the growth of cross-cultural communicative competence and proficiency by striving to become aware of various cultures and accepting the diversity that they bring to the educational system.

REFERENCES

American Council on Education. (1988). *One-third of a nation: Report of the Commission on Minority Participation in Education and American Life*. Washington, DC: Author.

Andrews, R. (1987). On leadership and student achievement. *Educational leadership*. Alexandria, VA: Association for Supervision and Curriculum Development.

Borman, K. M., & Spring, J. H. (1984). *Schools in central cities: Structure and process*. New York: Longman.

Budoff, M. (1987). Measures for assessing learning potential. In C. Schneider Lidz (Ed.), *Dynamic assessment: An interactional approach to evaluating learning potential* (pp. 173–195). New York: Guilford.

Campione, J. C., & Brown, A. L. (1987). Linking dynamic assessment with school achievement. In C. Schneider Lidz (Ed.), *Dynamic assessment: An interactional approach to evaluating learning potential* (pp. 82–115). New York: Guilford.

Cheng, L. L. (1989). Service delivery to Asian/Pacific LEP children: A cross-cultural framework. *Topics in Language Disorders, 9*, 1–14.

Cheng, L. L. (1990). The identification of communicative disorders in Asian-Pacific students. *Journal of Childhood Communicative Disorders, 13*(1), 113–119.

Cheng, L. L. (1991). *Assessing Asian language performance: Guidelines for evaluating LEP students* (2nd ed). Oceanside, CA: Academic Communication Associates.

Cheng, L. L., & Ima, K. (1989). *Understanding the immigrant Pacific Islander*. San Diego: Los Amigos Research Associates.

Cheng, L. L., & Ima, K. (1990). *Understanding the Filipino immigrant*. San Diego: Los Amigos Research Associates.

Chu, H. (1990). *The role of the Korean language in the bilingual programs in the United States*. Paper presented at the Asian Language Conference, Hsi-Lai Temple, Hacienda Heights, CA.

Damico, J. S. (1990). Descriptive assessment of communicative ability in limited-English-proficient students. In E. V. Hamayan & J. S. Damico (Eds.), *Limiting bias in the assessment of bilingual students* (pp. 157–217). Austin, TX: Pro-Ed.

Eggleston, K. (1977). *The sociology of the school curriculum*. London: Routledge & Kegan Paul.

Erickson, J., & Iglesias, A. (1986). Speech and language disorders in Hispanics. In O. Taylor (Ed.), *Nature of communication disorders in culturally and linguistically diverse populations* (pp. 181–217). Austin, TX: Pro-Ed.

Feuerstein, R. (1980). *Instrumental enrichment: An intervention program for cognitive modifiability*. Baltimore: University Park Press.

Feuerstein, R., Rand, Y., Jensen, M. R., Kaniel, S., & Tzuriel, D. (1987). Prerequisites for assessment of learning potential: The LPAD model. In C. Schneider Lidz (Ed.), *Dynamic assessment: An interactional approach to evaluating learning potential* (pp. 35–51). New York: Guilford.

Galang, R., Noble, V., & Halog, L. (1985). *Assessment of Filipino speaking limited-English-proficient students with special needs*. Unpublished manuscript.

Gardner, R. W., Robey, B., & Smith, P. C. (1985). Asian Americans: Growth, change, and diversity. *Population Bulletin, 40*, 1–44.

Gutierrez-Clellen, V. (1991). *A pluralistic approach to assessment of children's oral narratives: Clinical implication*. Unpublished manuscript.

Ima, K., & Labovitz, E. (1991). *Changing ethnic racial student composition and test performances: Taking account of increasing student diversity*. Paper presented at the annual meeting of the Pacific Sociological Association, Irvine, CA.

Ima, K., & Rumbaut, R. (1989). Southeast Asian refugees in American schools: A comparison between limited-English-proficient (LEP) and fluent-English-proficient (FEP) students. *Topics in Language Disorders, 9*, 54–75.

Kayser, H. (1991). *Cultural-linguistic diversity among Hispanic populations and associated communication disorders*. Presentation at the conference on teaching cultural-linguistic diversity in the graduate curricula of speech-language pathology and audiology, Hunter College of The City University of New York.

Kim, R. H. (1978). *Understanding Korean people, language, and culture*. Bilingual Education Resource Series. Olympia, WA: Office of the State Superintendent of Public Instruction. (ERIC Document Reproduction Service No. ED 201 714)

Kitano, M. K. (1991). A multicultural education perspective on serving the culturally diverse gifted. *Journal for the Education of the Gifted, 15*(1), 4–19.

Ma, L. J. (1985). Cultural diversity. In A. K. Dutt (Ed.), *Southeast Asia: Realm of contrast*. Boulder, CO: Westview.

Maker, C. J., & Schiever, S. W. (Eds.). (1989). *Critical issues in gifted education. Vol. 2: Defensible programs for cultural and ethnic minorities*. Austin, TX: Pro-Ed.

Monzon, R. I., (1984). *The effects of the family environment on the academic performance of Filipino-American college students*. Unpublished master's thesis, San Diego State University, San Diego, CA.

Nadeau, A. (1991, April). *Assessment strategies in the Next Century Schools Project*. Symposium of the annual conference of the American Educational Research Association, Chicago, IL.

Ogbu, J., & Matute-Bianchi, M. (1986). Understanding sociocultural factors: Knowledge, identity, and school adjustment. In *Beyond language: Social and cultural factors in schooling language minority students* (pp. 73–142). Los Angeles: Evaluation, Dissemination and Assessment Center, California State University.

O'Hare, W. P., & Felt, J. C. (1991, February). Asian Americans: America's fastest growing minority group. *Population Trends and Public Policy*. (Monograph No. 19). Washington, DC: Population Reference Bureau.

Ortiz, A. (1990). *Language acquisition vs. language disorders*. Paper presented at the second annual Bilingual Special Education Conference, San Diego County Office of Education, San Diego, CA.

Rumbaut, R., & Ima, K. (1988). *The adaptation of Southeast Asian refugee youth: A comparative study*. San Diego: San Diego State University.

Trueba, H. (1989). *Raising silent voices*. New York: Newberry House.

Tseng, O. (1990). *The psychological dimension of bilingual language acquisition*. Paper presented at the Asian Language Conference, Hsi-Lai Temple, Hacienda Heights, CA.

Valverde, L. A. (1988). Principals creating better schools in minority communities. *Education and Urban Society, 20*, 319–326.

Zappia, I. A. (1989). Identification of gifted Hispanic students: A multidimensional view. In C. J. Maker & S. W. Schiever (Eds.), *Critical issues in gifted education. Vol. 2: Defensible programs for cultural and ethnic minorities* (pp. 19–26). Austin, TX: Pro-Ed.

CHAPTER 4

Nonstandardized Instruments for the Assessment of Mexican-American Children for Gifted/Talented Programs

Jaime H. García

Identification of Mexican-American children for programs for the gifted and talented remains problematic. As a result, students from this population are underrepresented in gifted programs throughout the United States. For example, in Texas, where Hispanics make up 34% of the school population, only 18% of students identified for gifted programs in the 1990–1991 school year were Hispanic (Texas Education Agency, 1991). This discrepancy is due in large part to the problems associated with the use of traditional assessment procedures—such as achievement and group intelligence tests—for the identification of these children and to the manner in which data are evaluated by decision makers in the schools.

Equating giftedness with genius or prodigy also contributes to the underrepresentation of Mexican-American students and students from other ethnic and cultural groups for gifted programs. While researchers have attempted to refine and broaden the definition of giftedness, many classroom teachers and community members continue to equate giftedness with an IQ score of at least 130. In spite of these internalized definitions, broadened definitions that focus on behaviors associated with giftedness have been advocated for some time. Gallagher and Kinney (1974) reported five indicators of giftedness that resulted from a meeting of leaders in gifted education from various ethnic and cultural groups. These indicators included:

1. The ability to meaningfully manipulate a symbol system held valuable in a subculture.

2. The ability to think logically, given appropriate data.

3. The ability to use stored knowledge to solve problems.

4. The ability to reason by analogy.

5. The ability to extend or extrapolate knowledge to new situations or unique applications.

Close to 20 years later, these indicators are currently serving as the foundation of research on giftedness as a contruct being conducted at the University of Georgia, site of the National Research Center on the Gifted and Talented.

For Mexican-American students, as well as children from other ethnic and cultural groups, the major obstacle in showing potential, which is the cornerstone of gifted programs, is the overreliance on intelligence tests and other verbally loaded instruments that may be inappropriate for this population (Melesky, 1985). Kamin (cited in Torrance, 1982) stated that intelligence tests would never have been accepted in the United States if there had been no bias against minority populations. Research (Boyle, 1987; Gerken, 1985) has shown that intelligence tests, as well as achievement measures, are biased against children for whom English is not their primary language. However intelligence tests are often the only criteria considered when identifying students for gifted programs. Even when multiple criteria are used, there is often a tendency to ignore qualitative or anecdotal data in favor of test scores such as group-administered intelligence tests and achievement tests..

In addition, cultural differences in behavior, cognitive style, and learning style work against the identification of these children. Some behavior, such as cooperation in completing academic tasks, is often viewed as laziness or academic inferiority by teachers (Delgado-Galtan & Trueba, 1985). Cognitive styles in conflict with those represented in classrooms in the United States further add to the perception that Mexican-American children are not good students (Ramírez, Herold, & Castañeda, 1974). Manifestations of characteristics associated with giftedness may be different in Mexican-American children, yet educators are seldom trained in identifying those behaviors except as they are observed in the majority culture. Thus, even with rating scales and other qualitative instruments, Mexican-American children tend to be nominated at a lower rate than children of the majority population (High & Udall, 1983).

In an effort to provide a better system for the identification of all potentially gifted children, current research advocates use of nonstandardized qualitative instruments and methods that provide a better profile of a child than do strict quantitative instruments such as achievement and intelligence tests. It is hoped that using both types of instruments will make identification procedures for gifted programs more equitable for Mexican-American children, as well as those from other ethnic and cultural groups. As a result of the conference report *Talent Delayed—Talent Denied: The Culturally Different Gifted Child* (Gallagher & Kinney, 1974) and other reports, many states now require that multiple criteria be used in the screening and identification process for gifted programs. Additionally, many states require multiple criteria to be used in the identification of gifted children, in addition to requiring that children score two standard deviations above the mean on intelligence tests or above the 90th or 95th percentile on achievement tests in order even to be considered for a gifted program. However, even when multiple criteria are used, the instruments selected tend to consist of subtests of achievement tests and group-administered intelligence tests.

This chapter discusses several assessment strategies that provide qualitative data to be used in the identification of gifted Mexican-American students. These instruments and procedures can be broken down into four categories: student production, informant data, language and cognitive style data, and data organization systems. Student production methods include portfolios and generic student products. Informant data include behavioral checklists, jot-downs, parent interviews, and peer nominations. Language and cognitive style data describe the roles of language proficiency assessment and cognitive style ratings. Data organization systems include a review of the student profile form as conceptualized by Frasier (1991) and a modified student profile form currently under development by the author.

STUDENT PRODUCTION

The Portfolio

A portfolio is a collection of student work, like that which an architect or photographer might develop. One format for implementing portfolios was formulated by Sandra Kaplan (n.d.-a) for the Texas Education Agency. The portfolio was used with a target population of young children for whom it was difficult to collect accurate quantitative data. It was seen as a useful tool with children from culturally and linguistically diverse backgrounds since the products contained in the portfolio did not have to depend on language or directly reflect academic achievement. Since its development, the portfolio has been recognized as a tool that can be used with children of any age.

The process of establishing a portfolio follows a definite pattern. First, a series of lessons is conducted to introduce students to the uses of a portfolio. Adjunct lessons often include some that assist students in identifying special abilities they have (Lubbock ISD, 1989). Directions are given for including an item in the portfolio. Since these activities are introductory in nature, they can be translated for various linguistic groups without affecting the quality of entries made to the portfolio. When a child elects to include an item in his or her portfolio, a form is attached on which the child explains what the item shows about his or her abilities. Six to eight items of the child's choosing are entered in the portfolio. This collection occurs over a period of 2 to 3 months, which provides a sense of the child's development. While some of the items may be added by teachers or parents, the majority of the items in the portfolio are selected by the child. This provides students with a way to present what they consider their best work. Further, this self-selection empowers them and assists in developing a healthy self-esteem.

The district portfolio evaluation committee evaluates portfolios on eight criteria that indicate creative or academically advanced behavior. The criteria suggested by Kaplan (n.d.-a) include the following:

- Unusual presentation of an idea
- Work advanced beyond age or grade level.
- Complex or intricate presentation of an idea.
- In-depth understanding of an idea or skill.
- Resourceful and/or clever use of materials.
- Evidence of support of research for the idea.
- Work organized to communicate effectively
- Evidence of high interest and perseverance.

The results of the consensus reached by the committee can be examined in terms of consistent characteristics the child exhibits or the overall quality of the portfolio. Since there are no standardized procedures for rating the portfolios, the committee's discussion of the characteristics exhibited is based on the local school population's manifestation of those characteristics and the consensus of the review committee given that context.

Research currently being conducted to examine the predictive validity of portfolios is showing that portfolios are a better predictor of future student achievement than most instruments (Johnsen, Ryser, & Dougherty, 1993). The identification procedures evaluated in Johnsen and colleagues' study included an intelligence test, a creativity test, teacher rating, and portfolios. A stepwise regression examined the accuracy of each instrument in predicting future achievement as shown by achievement test scores. The findings indicated that portfolios were a better predictor than the other instruments. However, the variance was small. It would appear that when properly implemented, the portfolio can be a valuable tool in the assessment of children from all populations for gifted programs.

Paulson and Paulson (1991) have aptly cautioned that when focus is placed on validity and reliability valuable information may be thrown out. Validity and reliability assume that what is being measured is linear when in fact human cognitive performance is a multidimensional phenomenon that occurs in context. Thus, the focus when evaluating portfolios should be on what is observed about a student's ability rather than whether there is rater agreement on what is observed. It is through the discussions and disagreements of those reviewing the portfolio that rich data are extracted.

Among the benefits of the portfolio are the limited use of language if necessary and its facility in allowing the child to self-select examples of his or her best work. Another benefit is that growth over time can be observed, since the items in a portfolio are collected over a period of at least 2 months. While the accompanying inclusion form requires some verbal skills, it can be completed in the language the child prefers; the teacher or another adult can assist in completing the form. Additionally, the form is used only to identify the item and understand the child's reasons for selecting the item; it is not evaluated along with the product.

Generic Products

Studies (Bernal & DeAvila, 1976; DeAvila & Havassy 1975) have found that gifted children perform at a higher level on Piagetian scales than children falling within the norm. Gifted children tend to exhibit higher cognitive functioning at an earlier age. Thus, analysis of tasks performed by children can discriminate between children classified as gifted and their peers (Bernal & DeAvila, 1976).

Consequently, another method of evaluating children's products involves using what can be termed *generic products*. With this process, children receive instruction for a particular activity. The screening and selection committee can then compare the products at a given grade level or school site. These products are designed to require advanced problem solving skills and thus show differences among students.

One lesson used in a summer program for gifted students from disadvantaged backgrounds required students to make as many categories as possible in a limited amount of time using geometric shapes of varying size, color, and thicknesses. Another required students to create a figure using toothpicks and jellybeans. The resulting products were then compared to those of other children within the same school environment and with developmental stages. Since these activities were not normed, a committee ranked a student's response in comparison to his or her peers at a specific grade level or school site. To use this method, directions on how to conduct the lesson should be scripted and detailed so that students in different classrooms receive the same instructions.

INFORMANT DATA

Behavioral Checklists

Behavioral checklists used in the identification process for gifted programs have by and large been considered ineffective in the hands of teachers. Accuracy in identification using teacher checklists ranges from 10% at the primary level to 50% at the high school level (Nelson, 1982). With training, however, a significant improvement in the quality of teacher evaluations has been noted. For Mexican-American children and children from other ethnic and cultural groups, the problem has been exacerbated by the linguistic, cultural, and socioeconomic factors that come into play.

Attempts to ameliorate this problem include checklists that are defined in terms of how children from various ethnic and cultural groups exhibit gifted behaviors. There is evidence that use of culture-specific or culture-sensitive checklists can improve the quality of data gathered on these children. One example of such an effort is the Gifted Behaviors at Home and School checklist (García, 1989), which was based on a review of the literature (Bernal, 1974, 1980; Renzulli, Smith, White, Callahan, & Hartmann, 1976; Tannenbaum, 1983; Torrance, 1977). It provides (a) an ongoing assessment and evaluation instrument that parents or teacher can use over time to look for those behaviors associated with giftedness, (b) a format for an annotated record of how those behaviors are manifested in children, and (c) examples of how children from diverse ethnic and cultural groups exhibit gifted behaviors in both school and home environments. Even though examples are provided, training in the use of this type of instrument is essential.

As with portfolios, these types of checklists are gaining acceptance as a useful tool in gathering data for assessment. However, High and Udall (1983) found that even in schools where the majority of the students are from another ethnic or cultural background, the children are nominated for gifted programs at a lower rate than children from the dominant culture. This, combined with the problems associated with teacher ratings, points to the need for training in the use of behavioral checklists in order to determine the best educational placement for children. Training should include, but not be limited to, models and definitions of giftedness, characteristics of gifted children, sociocultural differences, and behavioral indicators of giftedness for the children represented in varied populations.

Jot-Downs

Jot-downs are matrices with indicators of giftedness noted in each cell. As a child exhibits any of the behaviors on the matrix, the observer writes the child's name in the cell along with a brief description of how the indicator was exhibited. Like the behavioral checklist previously discussed, the jot-down (Kaplan, n.d.-b) provides an ongoing evaluation format. Based on indicators of giftedness found by various researchers (Renzulli et al., 1976; Tannenbaum, 1983), the jot-down provides a format for the teacher to observe a student's performance over time.

The simplicity of the jot-down has been noted as a strong point in that it allows the user to observe patterns in the traits a child exhibits. Jotting down a child's name on a matrix/grid as behaviors are observed allows patterns of behavior to be noted and evaluated. As with teacher rating forms, it is necessary to train users. The jot-down, like other nonstandardized measures, has yet to be evaluated empirically, although it has a strong theoretical foundation.

Jot-downs are also applicable in the home. Parents, if provided with instruction regarding the characteristics of children with potential and given examples of how those behaviors may be manifested, can use the jot-down to note behaviors associated with giftedness. Such examples of behaviors can be useful in assessing the child for services in a gifted program.

Parent Interviews

Although viewed with skepticism by educators, data collected from parents can provide insight into a child's abilities. In most cases, data collected from parents are disregarded in favor of data from other sources such as standardized test scores and teacher ratings. Some parents may find that the forms provided by schools to solicit information for evaluation of their child for a gifted program are vague or hard to understand. One method that has been proposed to collect information more accurately from parents is the interview.

Parent interviews have not commonly been utilized in the assessment of children for gifted programs. However, support for this method of gathering data comes from two sources. One is researchers in the field of gifted education, such as Bernal (1980), who suggested that gifted programs be based on how the community defines giftedness. The other is from research conducted in cultural anthropology, where the interview (Spradley, 1979) is an essential tool in gathering data. These two concepts point to the inclusion of a parent interview as a way of gathering data in the assessment of children for gifted programs. With children from backgrounds in which English is not the primary language, a parent interview allows consideration of the community and home environment in the evaluation.

The parent interview should ideally be conducted by community volunteers who are trained in the process of conducting interviews that focus on the child's characteristics and abilities. By having community members conduct the interview in the home, the comfort level of parents can be maintained, thereby making the data collected clearer and more useful. The use of community members to conduct interviews also ensures that the language used in framing questions is the language of the community. The process is an improvement on the usual parent checklists in that the interviewer can probe further and obtain data that may not arise from a checklist. A better profile of the child results, since items not addressed on a checklist can be considered. Patton (1990) has provided a valuable reference, giving a comprehensive view of the components and procedures to be followed in conducting an interview.

Several drawbacks can be identified in the use of this data-collection method. These include (a) the time-consuming nature of parent interviews, (b) training needed by interviewers, and (c) training needed by school personnel in analyzing the interviews. However, considering the benefits gained by conducting interviews both in terms of identification and implications for programming, the time required is well spent.

Peer Nomination

A much neglected source of information has been the child's peers. Without evidence to support the claim, many have felt that nomination by peers would be unreliable at all age levels and impossible to assess at the younger age levels. As this method is further investigated, evaluated, and refined, it may prove to be a valuable source of information. There is growing support for the inclusion of peer nomination in the assessment process. As any person who works with children can note, children accurately assess each other's abilities and can tell one much about their peers.

One particularly interesting peer nomination form was developed by the Nebraska State Office of Education (1984) for use with young children. The form assesses children's perceptions of their peers' creative abilities. Given a scenario such as the class finding a puppy, children are asked to identify those peers who would, among other things, (a) have the most original ideas for the puppy's name, (b) have the most diverse ideas for tricks the puppy could be taught, and (c) show the greatest leadership abilities. Initial findings from a study involving elementary-age children (Lopez & Orzechowski, 1990) indicate that this procedure does indeed offer an additional alternative.

COGNITIVE STYLE AND LANGUAGE

Perhaps one of the greatest needs in the assessment of Mexican-American children for gifted programs is the attention paid to cognitive style and language. Taylor (1990; personal communication, July 8, 1992) suggested that language is a great determiner of the perception of an individual's ability. As such, he suggested that lack of knowledge, sensitivity and appreciation of diverse communication styles can result in inappropriate assessment. For Mexican-American children whose first language is not English, observed scores are at times the result of lack of experience with English rather than lack of comprehension of ideas and concepts (de Bernard, 1985).

With this in mind, it is essential that language proficiency in both English and Spanish be obtained from Mexican-American students in order to look at data collected within the linguistic context. Examination of the types of errors made in phonology and semantics on a discrete point test such as the Language Assessment Scales (LAS) (DeAvila & Duncan, 1981) may provide a window through which standardized scores on language tests can be viewed effectively.

A pragmatic analysis of the child's language production (Damico, 1985), either written or oral (dictated), may also assist in the interpretation of data collected. Unlike discrete point tests, pragmatics examines the way an individual uses language. An understanding of this may be useful when the assessment process includes writing samples, standardized intelligence test scores that were verbally loaded, and/or achievement subtests with strong language-dependent components.

Another culture-bound attribute is cognitive style. Field dependence/sensitivity, as well as other aspects of cognitive style, were examined among Mexican Americans by Ramirez and Castañeda (1974). Their research suggests that the teaching styles used in the classroom may not be congruent with the cognitive styles of Mexican-American students. Beyond having implications in classroom practices, this body of research has implications for assessment. If an instrument requires the use of a particular cognitive style and the cognitive style of the child is different, observed scores may be skewed.

As with language proficiency assessment, determining aspects of the cognitive style of Mexican-American children may provide a context from which to interpret standardized test scores. Ramirez and Castañeda (1974) provided rating forms for the observation of field-independent and field-sensitive behaviors in children. The use of this or other measures should be an integral part of the assessment of Mexican-American children for gifted programs.

DATA ORGANIZATION SYSTEMS

Student Profile Form

The student profile form (Frasier, 1990, 1991) has been modified in a variety of ways. Profile forms such as the F-TAP (Frasier, 1991) were developed in response to the rigidity found in matrix forms, where scores are assigned weighted point values based on score ranges. The common thread among profile forms is that they allow the plotting of standardized scores on the form. Scores that are not standardized can be plotted on the profile by determining where the score falls on a given continuum. By plotting a given score in relation to other scores, the integrity of all the scores is maintained. It also makes it possible to observe patterns across various instruments that assess varying areas of ability.

For Mexican-American students and students from backgrounds in which English is not the primary language, the profile form allows the identification committee to view the data in more holistic terms and to recognize whether additional data should be collected in any of the areas being assessed. If used as intended, the profile form can reduce bias in the assessment of Mexican-American children. Results from a district using the profile approach have shown that the method is more equitable than the matrix approach (Anthony, 1990). Keller (1990) has noted, however, that there may still be tendency to focus on test scores.

The Q^2 Profile Form

Test scores tend to drive decisions affecting educational programs for children. In an effort to resolve the issue of treating qualitative data in a manner that gives it the weight of quantitative data, the Quantitative/Qualitative (Q^2) Profile form is currently under development (see Figure 4-1). The Q^2 differs from other profiles in that anecdotal or narrative data are kept in narrative form. Further, qualitative data are reviewed before quantitative data. This helps ensure that quantitative data (e.g., test scores) do not influence the committee's interpretation of nonstandardized data. Keller (1990) found that this procedure allows selection committees to discuss qualitative data without the influence of the standardized test scores. The Q^2 combines quantitative and qualitative data. This results in the ability to aggregate data without losing the integrity of the individual instruments, one of the strong points of the profile approach to data organization.

The Q^2 is a two-sided form. Demographic data are found on the side that provides space for the qualitative data. Qualitative data are written as narrative in the space provided on the left side of the form. The committee's observations of student strengths uncovered in the assessment, and/or frequently observed behaviors, are sketched in the interpretation column on the right. After discussion of these data, the quantitative scores found on the reverse side of the form can be examined. Figure 4-1 shows the types of instruments that lend themselves to narrative evaluation.

The side of the form used to plot quantitative scores is divided into several sections. Space is provided to comment or to note observations made during the testing session. These observations, when considered along with the demographic data found on the form, can assist a committee in better interpreting the scores. The other sections are used to identify the type of score being entered (e.g., standard score, percentile), the raw score, and the plotted score. Scores obtained on any given instrument can then be viewed in light of observations made while testing.

Once both types of data have been reviewed, the committee can make a decision. The decision can range from *selection* to *need more data* to *does not qualify at this time*. Forms should be kept and further data added if a student is again nominated for a gifted program. To be most useful, the form should remain a dynamic means of data collection.

Qualitative data must be examined holistically and remain in narrative form if they are to provide worthwhile information. Qualitative data should be examined before test scores to allow strengths to be noted. Such data should be kept in narrative form in order to elicit discussion of

FIGURE 4-1

Q^2

Name _____ Date _____ Ethnicity _____

Language Proficiency (L1/L2) _____ Years in Bilingual Education (circle) Pre-K K 1 2 3 4 5 6 7 8 9 10 11 12

Migrant (Y/N) _____   Special Education Services _____

Data	Analysis
Product Evaluation Narrative:	1. 2. 3. 4. 5. 6.
Parent Interview Narrative:	1. 2. 3. 4. 5. 6.
Peer Nomination Narrative:	1. 2. 3. 4. 5. 6
Rating Scales Narrative:	1. 2. 3. 4. 5. 6.
Additional Data:	1. 2. 3. 4. 5. 6.

53

FIGURE 4-1 (continued)

Q²

Name _____

	Raw Score	Type of Score	0.....99 0.....49 <mean	100...108 50......68 mean–.5s	109...116 69.....83 .5s–1s	117..124 84......92 1sd–1.5s	125+ 93......99 >1.5s
		Instruments					
C	INSTRUMENT: _____ Admin Date: _____ Comments:						
R							
I	INSTRUMENT: _____ Admin Date: _____ Comments:						
T							
E	INSTRUMENT: _____ Admin Date: _____ Comments:						
R							
I	INSTRUMENT: _____ Admin Date: _____ Comments:						
A							

Adapted from Mary M. Frasier by Jaime H. García

strengths when reviewing the data. Finally, the data collected should be used for making programming and curriculum decisions for students.

CONCLUSION

A major concern in assessment has been variance in standardized scores between and among populations. Education has been centered on the concepts of reliability and validity as the tools by which decisions are made, thus neglecting valuable assessment data. Using instruments built on linear sequential models (i.e., statistics) to assess multidimensional nonlinear phenomena (i.e., human beings) has resulted in decisions that are questionable at best. Gleick (1987) stated that "a statistician uses the bell-shaped curve the way an internist uses a stethoscope, as the instrument of first resort" (p. 84). In education, the bell-shaped curve as applied to instrumentation has been used as the first and last resort.

Perhaps chaos theory provides a more appropriate way of viewing the assessment process. Gleick (1987) defined chaos as "a science of process rather than state, of becoming rather than being" (p. 5). Chaos theory suggests that an organism must be looked at as a whole. The theory relies on the study of deterministic patterns that are nonlinear. Given the nature of human beings, the assessment of children for gifted programs should be multidimensional. The singular reliance on quantitative measures provides only limited information. Reliability and validity in standardized instruments allow for comparison, but they provide only a limited understanding of a child's abilities. Examining performance patterns based on both quantitative and qualitative data is essential in assessment. Using both quantitative and nonstandardized procedures provides a more comprehensive view of a child's abilities.

As noted, identification of gifted children from the Mexican-American population remains problematic. The move toward including qualitative data along with quantitative data should provide for a more accurate assessment of children who exhibit gifted characteristics. The shift from the exclusive use of quantitative data assists in developing a more thorough and equitable assessment of children because it examines the whole child and not only those narrow areas assessed by standardized tests. While the practices noted here are *appropriate* for all populations, they are more likely to be *essential* for the equitable assessment of Mexican-American children for gifted programs. Continued reliance on standardized test scores can only result in the continued underrepresentation of these students in gifted programs.

Each of the categories of data presented offers viable alternatives and additions to current assessment procedures. Student production procedures allow for the demonstration of potential through performance over time. Informant data, eliciting valuable information from parents, can assist in ensuring that children are not excluded from programs for the gifted due to linguistic and/or cultural differences. Additionally, data gathered from peers, as well as teachers who have been trained to observe behaviors characteristic of gifted children in their communities, can provide another avenue in the assessment process. Assessment of language proficiency and cognitive style can provide a framework from which to view observed performance. Since these procedures use the language with which the child is most comfortable, the process is more equitable for Mexican-American children, as well as those from other underrepresented populations. As these methods of gathering data are studied further and gain acceptance as a viable and valuable source of information, Mexican-American children and children from other cultural and ethnic groups will have greater opportunities to demonstrate their potential.

Profile forms that allow for a more global view of how a child performs on various instruments are also more equitable for Mexican-American children and others from linguistically and culturally different backgrounds. As profile forms are refined, and as they increase in use, children will be evaluated as individuals rather than as a set of numbers on a matrix that fails to take into account the child's unique abilities.

With the continued discrepancies between the number of Mexican-American children and children from other cultural and ethnic groups enrolled in public schools and the number of those children participating in programs for potentially gifted children, the investigation and use of these techniques may provide for the identification of children who are not receiving an education commensurate with their abilities.

Equity and *excellence* are not mutually exclusive terms. Methods of identifying Mexican-American gifted children are available, and they do not dilute the quality of programs for gifted students. Research has shown that students identified for gifted programs by means other than intelligence tests perform as well as those identified through the use of intelligence tests (Torrance, 1982). The field of gifted education will continue to be accused of being elitist if children from culturally and linguistically diverse populations continue to be missed. The challenge is to employ and refine procedures to ensure that children are assessed in such a manner that their educational needs are identified and addressed.

The demographics of the United States are rapidly changing. The continued underidentification of gifted students who are Mexican American, as well as those from other cultural and ethnic groups, can only result in depressed productivity and innovation in the United States. While this loss is one that affects society, it is a greater loss to the child whose potential is not realized because the system fails to meet students' needs. Cummins (1989) quoted Mary Ashworth, who, at a teaching English as a second language (TESL) conference in Ontario, stated:

> The roots of the term *education* imply drawing out children's potential, making them more than they were; however, when children come to school fluent in their primary language and they leave school essentially monolingual in English, then our schools have negated the meaning of the term *education* because they have made the children *less* than they were. (p. xii)

REFERENCES

Anthony, T. S. (1990). The identification of gifted disadvantaged African-American students. *CAG Communicator, 10*(3), 9–11.

Bernal, E. M. (1974). Gifted Mexican American children: An ethnoscientific perspective. *California Journal of Educational Research, 25*(5), 261–273.

Bernal, E. M. (1980). *Methods of identifying gifted minority students.* (Report No. 72). Princeton, NJ: Educational Resources Information Center.

Bernal, E. M., & DeAvila, E. (1976, May). *Assessing gifted and average children with the Cartoon Conservation Scales.* Paper presented at the annual meeting of the National Association for Bilingual Education, San Antonio, TX.

Boyle, J. P. (1987). Intelligence, reasoning, and language proficiency. *The Modern Language Journal, 71*(3), 277–283.

Cummins, J. (1989). *Empowering minority students: A framework for intervention.* Sacramento: California Association for Bilingual Education.

Damico, J. S. (1985). Clinical discourse analysis: A functional approach to language assessment. In C. Simen (Ed.), *Communication skills and classroom success: Assessment of language-learning disabled students* (pp. 165–204). San Diego: College-Hill.

DeAvila, E. A., & Duncan, S. E. (1981). *Language Assessment Scales.* San Rafael: Linguametrics Group.

DeAvila, E. A., & Havassy, B. (1975). Piagetian alternatives to IQ: Mexican-American study. In N. Hobbs (Ed.), *Issues in the classification of exceptional children.* San Francisco: Jossey-Bass.

de Bernard, A. E. (1985). Why José can't get into the gifted class: The bilingual child and standardized reading tests. *Roeper Review, 8*(2), 80–82.

Delgado-Galtan, C., & Trueba, H. T. (1985). Ethnographic study of the participant structures in task completion: Reinterpretation of "handicaps" in Mexican children. *Learning Disability Quarterly, 8,* 67–75.

Frasier, M. M. (1990). *Assessment of minority students for gifted programs.* Unpublished manuscript, The University of Georgia, Athens.

Frasier, M. M. (1991). Disadvantaged and culturally diverse gifted students. *Journal for the Education of the Gifted, 14*(3), 234–245.

Gallagher J., & Kinney, L. (1974). *Talent delayed—talent denied: The culturally different gifted child. A conference report*. Reston, VA: Foundation for Exceptional Children.

García, J. H. (1989). *Gifted behaviors at school and home in minority children*. Unpublished manuscript. Austin: Texas Education Agency.

Gerken, K. C. (1985). Performance of Mexican-American children on intelligence tests. *Exceptional Children, 44*, 438–443.

Gleick, J. (1987). *Chaos: Making a new science*. New York: Penguin.

High, M. H., & Udall, A. J. (1983). Teacher rating of students in relation to ethnicity of students and school ethnic balance. *Journal for the Education of the Gifted, 6*(3), 154–166.

Johnsen, S. K., Ryser, G., & Dougherty, E. (1993). The validity of product portfolios in the identification of gifted students. *Gifted International: A Talent Development Journal, 8*(1), 40–43.

Lubbock Independent School District. (1989). *Pull-ins*. Lubbock, TX: Author.

Kaplan, S. (n.d.-a). *Academic portfolio*. Austin: Texas Education Agency.

Kaplan, S. (n.d.-b). *The jot down*. Austin: Texas Education Agency.

Keller, M. (1990). Holistic identification of potentially gifted students: An alternative to the matrix. *Instructional Leadership, 12*(5), 4–7.

Lopez, R. M., & Orzechowski, D. (1990, October). *Using peer nominations in screening for gifted students from diverse cultural backgrounds*. Paper presented at The Council for Exceptional Children Symposium on Culturally Diverse Exceptional Learners, Albuquerque, NM.

Melesky, T. J. (1985). Identifying and providing for the Hispanic gifted child. *NABE Journal, 9*(3), 43–56.

Nebraska State Department of Education. (1984). Peer identification—Creativity—Elementary. In J. A. Platow (Ed.), *A handbook for identifying the gifted/talented* (pp. 125–126). Ventura, CA: Ventura County Superintendent of Schools.

Nelson, H. (1982). The identification of black and Hispanic talented and gifted students—grades K through 6: In search of an educational standard. In *Identifying and educating the disadvantaged gifted/talented: Proceedings from the Fifth National Conference on Disadvantaged Gifted/Talented* (pp. 63–90). Ventura, CA: Ventura County Superintendent of Schools.

Patton, M. Q. (1990). *Qualitative methods in research and evaluation* (2nd ed.). Newbury Park, CA: Sage.

Paulson, F. L., & Paulson, P. R. (1991, April). *The ins and outs of using portfolios to assess performance (rev. ed.)*. Paper presented at the Joint Annual Meeting of the National Council of Measurement in Education and the National Association of Test Directors, Chicago, Illinois. (ERIC Document Reproduction Service No. ED 334 250)

Ramírez, M., Herold, P. L., & Castañeda, A. (1974). *Field sensitivity and field independence in children*. Austin, TX: Dissemination Center for Bilingual/Bicultural Education.

Renzulli, J. S., Smith, L. H., White, A. J., Callahan, C. M., & Hartmann, R. K. (1976). *Scales for rating the behavioral characteristics of superior students*. Wethersfield, CT: Creative Learning.

Spradley, J. P. (1979). *The ethnographic interview*. New York: Holt, Rinehart, & Winston.

Tannenbaum, A. J. (1983). *Gifted children: Psychological and educational perspectives*. New York: Macmillan.

Taylor, O. L. (1990). *Cross-cultural communication: An essential dimension of effective education*. Washington, DC: Mid-Atlantic Equity Center.

Texas Education Agency. (1991). [Public Education Information Management System]. Austin, TX: Author.

Torrance, E. P. (1977). *Discovery and nurturance of giftedness in the culturally different*. Reston, VA: The Council for Exceptional Children.

Torrance, E. P. (1982). Misconceptions about creativity in gifted education: Removing the limits on learning. In *Curricula for the gifted: Selected proceedings from the First National Conference on Curriculum for the Gifted* (pp. 59–74). Ventura, CA: Ventura County Superintendent of Schools.